Honestly, there would be fewer suicides to talk about if there was more honest talk about the ones that have already occurred. This book is an important part of a conversation that must be held. Lives hang in the balance.

—Robert Benson, author, *Home by Another Way*

Harold Ivan Smith courageously guides us on a spiritual exploration of suicide in his pioneering book *A Long-Shadowed Grief*. He probes shadows, secrets, and silences, bringing us into a helpful light.

—The Rev. Canon Malcolm Boyd, author,
Are You Running with Me, Jesus?

Suicide grief takes us to the extremes—anger, guilt, fear, loneliness, spiritual despair. With stories, quotes, information, and friendship, Smith steps into these extremes with the greatest extreme: The wide-sweeping love of God that meets all of us along the way of this rough journey. This book is a gift to the bereaved as well as to those who provide care and support.

—Rev. Richard B. Gilbert, PhD, CT, executive director,
The World Pastoral Care Center

In the utter desolation that is suicide and its aftermath—and for which there *are* no comforting words—Harold Ivan Smith has written words of honesty, truth, insight, sensitivity, hope, and spiritual care that illumine the long dark shadows. I deeply believe that "naming" all aspects of those dark and hard places, which this book helps us do, invites God into and makes holy the place of our desolation; God thus becomes our Hand and Guide as we day by day inch toward our futuring. Smith's words help greatly to give meaning and direction to that walk, and are a resource of help and hope that I strongly recommend.

—Jodie Johnson, survivor;
wife of Bishop David E. Johr

The journey of the suicide survivor can be long and complicated. Harold Ivan Smith has written an incredible resource, one that can aid survivors on this unknown path they have been forced upon. This is a resource all suicide survivors should read because each person can benefit in some way from Smith's soothing words.

—Michelle Linn-Gust, M.S., American Association of Suicidology, Survivor Division Chair; author, *Do They Have Bad Days in Heaven? Surviving the Suicide Loss of a Sibling*

This is the most inspirational book on grief from a Christian perspective that I have ever read. Smith's approach is spiritual in a most non-judgmental way. It is inclusive, grace-filled, and even his prose is poetic and comforting.

—Janice Winchester Nadeau, PhD, author, *Families Making Sense of Death*

A Long-Shadowed Grief is an extraordinarily helpful guidebook for persons who have been bereaved by suicide and for individuals who seek to help such persons. It tackles a wide range of issues that surround this very difficult form of death and is informed throughout by a distinctively spiritual and caring point of view.

—Charles A. Corr, PhD, board of directors, Hospice Institute of the Florida Suncoast

A Long-Shadowed Grief

COWLEY PUBLICATIONS is a ministry of the brothers of the Society of Saint John the Evangelist, a monastic order in the Episcopal Church. Our mission is to provide books and resources for those seeking spiritual and theological formation. COWLEY PUBLICATIONS is committed to developing a new generation of writers and teachers who will encourage people to think and pray in new ways about spirituality, reconciliation, and the future.

A Long-Shadowed Grief

Suicide and
Its Aftermath

HAROLD IVAN SMITH

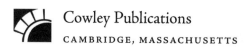

Cowley Publications
CAMBRIDGE, MASSACHUSETTS

Library of Congress Cataloging-in-Publication Data

Smith, Harold Ivan, 1947–
A long-shadowed grief : suicide and its aftermath / Harold Ivan Smith.
    p.   cm.
Includes bibliographical references.
ISBN-13: 978-1-56101-281-7 (pbk. : alk. paper)
ISBN-10: 1-56101-281-5 (pbk. : alk. paper)
    1. Bereavement—Religious aspects—Christianity. 2. Grief—Religious aspects—Christianity. 3. Consolation. 4. Suicide—Religious aspects—Christianity. 5. Spirituality. I. Title.

    BV4905.3.S633   2006
    248.8'66—dc22

                                                           2006021940

Cover design: Gary Ragaglia
Interior Design: Ann Sudmeier

This book was printed in the United States of America on acid-free paper.

Cowley Publications
4 Brattle Street
Cambridge, Massachusetts 02138
800-225-1534 • www.cowley.org

The important thing is not that you suicided.
The important thing is that you lived!

In memory of Wilma McDaniels
1938 – 1974

Robert A. Neimeyer, PhD

Suicide survivor who has used his loss
to enlarge the understanding of grief counselors

Table of Contents

A Long-Shadowed Grief

Introduction

Eighty-seven.
Every day eighty-seven individuals, in this country,
with names and faces, a family of some configuration,
friends and colleagues, end their lives.
Suicide, whether planned or compulsive, anticipated or shocking,
initiates the long shadow on survivors left to wander
across the fragile landscapes of the heart
toward a magic kingdom called "Answerland."
Suicide, like a volcano's lava flow, changes
everything in its path.
—Harold Ivan Smith

> Early, provisional meanings of the death tend to be revised
> as the reality of living with loss raises new questions and
> undermines old answers.
> —Robert Neimeyer[1]

Some survivors of suicide weave well-rehearsed questions—we might call them "why's"—into the fabric of their life narratives. To know a person as a survivor is to know of the suicide that has changed their lives, although not necessarily by its details. Some survivors divide life into two segments: *before* the shadow of death, and *after* the shadow, so that a suicide is the definitive moment of their existence.

Some survivors weep or wonder their why's into pillows, journals, chat rooms, shot glasses, syringes, pills, work, sex, busyness, and religiosity, seeking relief from the stalking accusations that menace their days, the indictments that terrorize the nights: "If *only* I had . . . perhaps, I *should* have. . . ." Some will go to their graves exhausted from wondering, "Why?" or "WHY!!!?," from asking what more they could have done, or said, or been that would have prevented the upheaval of their narrative.

Suicide, like a tsunami, rearranges the emotional shoreline forever. No one goes "back to normal." With God's grace, in time, a survivor creates a new normal.

Suicide alters the stories we tell others about ourselves, and the stories that we tell ourselves. Sorrow is a constant companion. Some survivors wince when someone asks, "How many children do you have?" or "Are you married?" or "Are your parents still living?" A simple question stings like a snapped towel in a locker room. Some answer, "He/she *died*," but those who listen closely hear the asterisk in the voice, the note of unspoken pain.

Unfortunately, some survivors have individuals on the margins of their lives who believe it is time—*past time*—for them to "move on," to "get over it," to arrive at the final "stage" of acceptance. Some unleash an accusatory tone of voice: "She has *never* gotten over it" or "He is *still* grieving!" These critical statements suggest that the mourner has somehow failed, as if he or she has earned the grade of "Incompetent Griever." To some, keeping grief after a suicide is a character flaw. Even more painfully, a few wonder what kind of husband or wife, mother or father, brother or sister, you are, you were, if a loved one took their life.

Sometimes the most accurate answer is, "Beats me." And it does beat the soul. The constant "whying" bruises the soul, but never discolors the skin for others to see.

Authors write from their own narratives, from the stories they have learned from their own lives. Just so, I write this book in the long shadow of grief, thirty-one years after the trigger was pulled.

I am not an expert on suicide. I am a survivor who believes in attending to one's soul. Spirituality is more than a buzzword, and the spiritual demands in our lives are real. While excellent books on suicide or spirituality are plentiful, this book brings those two fields together. To speak about the spirits of survivors, I want to ask two central questions: How can one live a spiritual life as a suicide survivor? In what ways is faith permanently altered by suicide, and by the stigma attached to it?

My Cousin Wilma

What would become the unmentionable thread in my maternal family narrative happened on a hot June night in 1974. Wilma, my kind, troubled cousin, took one of my uncle's guns—the one he recommended she use if she "intended to do a *thorough* job"—and ended her life in a car parked at a local grocery store. I responded groggily to my mother's telephone call early the next morning, "What possessed her to do *that?*" (A common query in our family's language.)

Mother abruptly ended the conversation with, "I'll call back when I know more." She wished only to transmit the news, not to unleash her well-rehearsed lament against her brother, "I always told him keeping all those guns in the house that someday somebody was going to get hurt!"

Mother knew that Wilma's death had little to do with guns—my uncle's arsenal only made it easier for Wilma to die by suicide. Most of the family—at least the women—knew that Wilma's death was not an impulsive act.

Three decades later, when I began asking questions, my aunt told me that my grandfather had often pointed to a particular tree on the farm and said, "That's the tree I am going to hang myself from. . . . You'll get up some morning, and find me swinging in the breeze." My aunt's story provided a missing piece of the puzzle of my cousin's death.

It would be years before I would know more, because my family was reluctant to speak clearly about Wilma's suicide. In our vernacular, my relatives would say, "Well, there's more to *that* story . . ." (a statement that was like bait to a hungry fish). But my decision to write this book, coupled with the death of Wilma's stepfather, my uncle, intensified my questions. Looking back on what I now know, I feel like a fool for never having tallied two and two to get four. My math was constricted by the presumption that tragedy could not really be a part of my life, at least not in the way I discovered—"Not in *my* family!"

To be frank, incest was not appropriate for polite table discussion in our family. To avoid the horror and humiliation of the word, conversations were always strained in my mother's family for fear that someone would "say the wrong thing" and create a verbal mêlée. Whatever prompts a suicide, families rarely find themselves able to speak honestly with each other about what happened. As I uncovered the difficult truth of my uncle and cousin's relationship, I found comfort in Margaret Truman's disclosure that her Grandfather Wallace's suicide was never discussed in *her* family. My situation wasn't unique; silence also runs in prominent families.

Looking back I hear pleas for help that I overlooked as an adolescent. Questions rose from my memories and hemorrhaged in my thinking as I wrote sections of this book immediately after my uncle's death. I wonder, for example, how God will deal with my uncle. He said he was ready to meet God. I hope so.

Other questions haunt me especially: How, for instance, could my family on so many occasions have argued furiously over minute points of religion while ignoring Wilma's pain—and her coerced sexual relationship with my uncle? (My uncle delighted in initiating many of those religious arguments with provocative statements like: "I was reading in my Bible that Jesus was married.") I wonder how he grieved those sexless nights after her death, as he turned into one bitter cantankerous fart.

Once family members knew that my Bible-quoting uncle was sleeping with his stepdaughter Wilma, why did his behavior go unchallenged? At what point did Wilma willingly become his bed partner, if ever? My uncle was the character who sabotaged the narrative of Wilma's life. It seems that at times she was little more than a marionette at the beck-and-call of his loins. So much was hidden in my family concerning their relationship. Now that they both have been laid to rest, a new revelation seems to appear at every turn. I wonder what other puzzlements will be raised and resolved in the aftermath of his death.

I remember Wilma's gifts to me on birthdays and Christmas. One, a toy gun, was taken years later when my home was burglarized. It was so special that I had never fired it. It was worth nothing economically, but to me it was invaluable. That toy was my last link with her. What might she have given me on future birthdays and Christmases had she lived? What might I have given her?

I have concluded that Wilma could think of no other way to end her pain than to die—a pain that had menaced her on hundreds of other nights before her last one, a pain that fed her decision to suicide when she could see no ray of hope on the horizon. She did not have friends. She did not work. She waited for my uncle to come home at the end of the day, every day.

Contemplating Suicide

I have seriously pondered ending my life. First, during a divorce—on days when I could not imagine a future rescripted without my permission. I did not want to die. I wanted the pain to end—the unbearable pain in the mind that Edwin Shneidman, the founder of suicidology, calls *psychache*.[2] I did not want to wait for healing in some distant moment. Shneidman has identified four main drivers of suicide: thwarted love, fractured control, assaulted self-image, and the rupture of a key relationship. I wrestled with all four. Every day was a psychological and spiritual brawl, only there was no referee to warn against unfair tactics and no bell to ring, mercifully, to end the fight.

Because of all the driving I did in my work as a college admissions counselor, I planned that my death would be reported like this: "He fell asleep driving on a secluded section of highway. . . ." That explanation would have been easier on my parents and friends than an acknowledgment that I had purposefully killed myself. More than once when friends asked, "You're not thinking of suicide, are you?" I lied.

Suicide can become attractive when living becomes unbearable.

One too many "bad days" become an intolerable life. Suicide lures with its siren promise: relief from the incessant mental and spiritual pain we are suffering.

Years later, in reflective moments, I audit the good gifts of life— and there have been many—especially the persons I have met, friendships I have known, the experiences I have had, the writing, the travel, and the achievements in my career. These are gifts I would have never experienced had I steered the car off the pavement one afternoon.

I am stronger for having danced with the temptation to end my life. My search for authentic spirituality began in that struggle.

I am more respectful of the limitations of human endurance of psychological, physiological, and spiritual pain because of my own suicidal contemplation.

I am more tolerant of answerless why's that loot our minds of peace and resolution.

I am more appreciative of the outrageous wideness of God's mercy.

I am spiritually stronger for learning to say, "I am Harold Ivan, a survivor of suicide."

In the end, I believe that I am more compassionate because I pondered suicide. I well know its seductive promise whispered in the dark despair of spiritual night. Recently, faced with a career-threat I was not initially certain I could face, let alone survive, in that midnight stillness, suicide whispered a "reasonable" answer in my mind. I moaned a brief prayer asking for sleep, believing that the situation would look different after rest. One byproduct of seriously pondering suicide is the conclusion rooted in my soul: within God's care, every experience in the human landscape is survivable. Unpleasant, unfair, humiliating, perhaps—but survivable. Through the experience I was reminded of the bullying power of impulse.

In a way I would never have anticipated, I owe my life to a fundamentalist radio preacher, the late John D. Jess. One afternoon as the deserted roadway across central Florida looked appropriate for the oft-imagined deed, I "happened" to switch radio stations and found the Chapel of the Air. In a moment that only God could have orchestrated, Brother Jess intersected my darkness:

Someone, *right now*, is thinking about ending your life. Someone *right now* believes suicide is the answer. That everyone would be "better off without me." Listen to me: do not do it! Suicide is *not* the answer. Jesus is!

I have, from time to time, wondered What if, in that broadcast, Brother Jess had chosen to expound on the Holiness Code in Leviticus, or the signs of prophesy-fulfillment in Nahum? What if I had tuned in to some talk-radio gasbag spewing cynicism, hopelessness, and foolishness? No way could I have imagined, in the providence of God, that years later I would be a guest of David Mains, Jess's successor as host of that broadcast.

Thinking Together

I am not an "authority" on suicide. In writing, I have weighted the trustable voices of recognized authorities, and I have listened to individuals dripping wet from the swirling baptismal waters of survival. Hopefully, my words, their words, your experience, and your thoughts as you read this book will collide and help us all find hope and grace in a world where suicide is growing.

No one can survive suicide alone. Survivors need the gifts others offer. Survivors need God, and God's friends (and often, some new friends). John Henson translated Paul: "God's Spirit gives one person the strength to do things nobody thought possible" (1 Corinthians 12:10, *Good as New*).[3] Think of something that often seems impossible: not just to survive, but to share survival tips with others. Edwin Shneidman, after a lifetime of studying suicide, offers two questions to keep at the ready when speaking with someone contemplating suicide or living in its aftermath: "Where do you hurt? How can I help?"[4] Thus my prayer has become: "God give me the strength and courage to face today's invitations and demands."

When a person close to us suicides, we become the inheritors of that person's final moment, their death. While life is forever changed, you can survive. As you mourn, you can let go of old assumptions and redesign your life. You can find loss a fertilizer for new dreams, and you can find hope in the ashes of your past aspirations. You can dare to believe that your emotional wasteland, in the prophetic words of Isaiah, "will blossom and bloom" (35:1–2). While taking a break from writing this chapter, I laughed out loud at a calligraphy that read, "The bulb has to go through a lot of dirt to become a blossom." And sometimes manure.

Survivors are not Lone Rangers. In a society that overly prizes rights, individualism, and "self-deliverance," the suicide statistics in this book may be low, since any numbers include only those recognized as suicide on a death certificate. If we knew the actual numbers of those who have suicided, we would be driven to vigorous prevention and enhanced care for survivors. In some places, in some families, the assessment "death by suicide" does not get officially made or recorded even though everyone *knows* the real cause of death. Some survivors, like Margaret Truman and Peter Selwyn, will not know the truth for many years, when someday someone lets "it" out of the bag. Nevertheless, their lives will be impacted by the suicide that has been kept hidden. In other places, stubborn individuals refuse to accept such a brutal conclusion as suicide and spend their lives chasing and embracing fictitious explanations: "He was cleaning the gun and it discharged." Not all fiction writers are novelists.

The significant question after a suicide is not only "Why?" That relentless question is limited in what it offers us; an answer would not bring the deceased back. Significant questions are also: "Now what, God? How do you want to bring a future out of this mess? How do you want to weave this reality into my spiritual life? How can you use this soul-wound to deepen me spiritually? How does a survivor live redemptively in the shadow of a loved one's suicide?"

The Apostle Paul framed words that seem appropriate encouragement for our time of grief: "Praise be the God and Father of our Lord Jesus Christ who comforts us in all our trials." Yet too many readers stop there, ignoring the comma in the biblical text. "So that," Paul continued, "we may share the comfort we have received with others" (2 Corinthians 1:4). Two millennia after Paul penned those words they offer a future to those who have survived "it," to those who are surviving it, to those who hope, somehow, to continue surviving it. Someone needs *your* words, *your* experience, *your* gained wisdom. Your yesterday is their today. Your today is a shoreline they doubt they can reach. As you read this, someone's nightmare has just begun. You may not be able to keep another from abandoning life and ending their pain. But your experience of survival can comfort those of us who have just begun to walk the survival trail. You can share with another who needs what you have learned. Only if we share the right turns, left turns, and u-turns of surviving can we accurately say, "I have survived this." Most of all, you can help new survivors grieve. It is all too easy for well-meaning, would-be comforters to mouth, or pen, the cliché "Time heals all wounds." Yet survivors know better. Katherine Ashenburg recalled uttering that worn platitude to a client who responded with great conviction, "Time doesn't heal. Grieving heals."[5] And our grief can help free another to also grieve.

One of the reasons it is important for us to support one another as survivors is because surviving suicide brings with it its own unique forms of grief. Psychologist Jack Jordan suggests that survivors of suicide may experience their bereavement in a way different from many other mourners:

+ Survivors seem to struggle more with making meaning of the death.
+ Survivors show higher levels of feelings of guilt, blame, and responsibility than those grieving other deaths.
+ Survivors acknowledge experiencing heightened feelings of rejection or abandonment by the loved one.
+ Survivors have more difficulty communicating with others about the loss.
+ Survivors tend to experience less support from their social network.[6]

Once we identify them, some of these peculiarities of survivors' grief are not difficult to imagine. Yet understandable as they are, feelings of abandonment and guilt are never easy to live with. The support we provide each other can go a long way to seeing us through our grief.

These experiences and feelings of loss, abandonment, and isolation have an effect on us. They shape who we are. They make us change. Thus, these same factors shape our spirituality as well. One of the primary tasks I have set for us in these pages is to encourage the changes in our spirituality due to this loss. It is important for us to give our grief space in our thinking and reflecting. Our souls will be better for it.

Survivors of Suicide: Two Definitions

Throughout this book I use two words that may strike some ears as slightly unusual. Allow me to explain my choice of these two words, central as they are to my hope for this book.

First, I will often deliberately use *suicide* as a verb. In my mind, explaining to you that my cousin suicided says something slightly other than telling you that she committed suicide. "Committed suicide" is sometimes perceived by survivors as pejorative, since one commits a homicide or some other public outrage. While I do not totally abandon this more common way of speaking, I do balance it with the verb I prefer to employ, "suicide." My usage is not innovative. It comes out of the lived experience, and shame, of many survivors. Admittedly, it may take some getting used to.

Second, I have worried that some readers will resist my use of the term *survivor*. I have even wondered if some will protest, "This author is only a 'second tier' survivor—he only lost a cousin, not a partner, or a parent, or a sibling, or a child." In my thought, I have relied on Victoria Alexander's definition. According to Alexander, survivors are:

[A]ll the people who experience [suicide] as a loss in their own lives. Survivors are family members, friends, lovers, colleagues, neighbors, schoolmates, therapists, and even whole communities. Ultimately, we are all survivors, in the sense that when one individual ends his or her life, that death is a loss for human society, for all of us collectively, as well as for some of us individually.[7]

I believe that the way I use both of these terms—*suicide* and *survivor*—can help us better understand the realities and possibilities following a person's choice to end their life. They are meant to speak the language of survivors, a language of experience, grief, dignity, and even hope.

There are many books, articles, monograms, journal articles, and videos on suicide. Perhaps you have sampled them or some have been given to you as gifts of comfort. What can I offer that others have not offered you? What insights can I bring to your reality? If you held this book and another in your hands in the aisles of a bookstore, what makes this book different, readable, believable?

I am a suicide survivor who hopes that you will keep the grief. That you will give your loss a voice and space. That you will give yourself time and space to grieve. That you will find words to voice your grief. That you will be wiser because of this tragic intrusion on your own life's narrative. That you will, in time, because of your struggles, fears, and angers, make the world safer. That in your own life you will reach a safe place, wiser and more humane.

Suicide is the long shadow over the lives and stories of its survivors. But a shadow can only exist if, somewhere, a bright light shines. God, according to 2 Samuel, "devises ways so that the banished do not remain estranged from him" (14:14). It is my hope that this book will be one of those ways.

Prayer: Creator, my loved one has ended earthly life.
  By that ending, my loved one
  has wounded me beyond comprehension.
  My assumptions, plans, dreams lay strewn
  along the corridors of my heart.
  See my wound. Hear my pain.
  Recognize my inability to find words of explanation.
  Invade my sorrow with hope. Amen.

Chapter 1

The Face of Suicide

It is not the statistics
that make suicide real.
It is when you know you love
one of those numbers.

God has special deeds for each of us to do in this world.
By doing them we repair that tiny corner of God's world
entrusted to us. We fulfill the meaning of our lives and become a blessing.

—*Rabbi Samuel Karff*[1]

Mary Paxton was awakened by her father in the middle of that night
in 1903, two weeks after her mother's death. "Mr. Wallace just shot
himself," he said. "Go see what you can do for Bess."[2] Mary dressed
quickly and walked to her best friend's house where she found a distraught Bess pacing the backyard. Mary paced beside Bess until dawn.
If someone had said to that 18-year-old Bess, as the long shadow first
fell across her life, "Someday you will be First Lady," could she have
believed them?

In 1944, Franklin Roosevelt chose a reluctant Harry Truman, U.S.
Senator from Missouri, as his vice-presidential running mate. Mrs.
Truman fretted that reporters would uncover her father's suicide and
use it against her husband, who was already portrayed as a political
hack beholden to the Missouri-based Pendergast political machine.

Mrs. Wallace, Bess's mother, who had been a virtual "prisoner of shame" since her husband's death, was also anxious.

When the Truman family, including 20-year-old daughter Margaret, returned home to Independence, Missouri after a campaign trip, Margaret's Aunt Natalie took it upon herself to inform her niece how Grandfather Wallace had died. Margaret, she reasoned, was old enough to know the truth, and Harry and Bess were too protective. If the suicide became public knowledge during the campaign, better for Margaret to have heard it first from a family member. In shock, Margaret sought out Vietta Garr, the family housekeeper, for confirmation. Garr acknowledged the truth with a nod. When Margaret asked her father, Truman exploded. "He seized my arm in a grip that he must have learned when he was wrestling calves and hogs around the farmyard. 'Don't you *ever* mention that to your mother.'"[3] Margaret later recalled:

> I wish I could tell you that years later I asked Mother if her anxiety about her father's death was the hidden reason for her opposition to Dad's nomination. But to the end of her life, I never felt free to violate the absolute prohibition Dad issued on that summer night in 1944. More than once, in these later years, I had hoped Bess would talk to me about her father, but she never did.[4]

The silence surrounding suicide aggressively recruits the next generation.

The Statistics

Due to the veil of shame and secrecy that often covers the truth of suicide, we might be surprised at how many people are affected by it. Some numbers offer a hint of the landscape of suicide.

31,655   Number of suicides in U.S. in 2002
287,000   Number of suicides each year in China[5]

1,000,000	Estimated number of suicides per year worldwide[6]
86.7	Number of suicides in U.S. per day
5,548	Number of individuals per year over age 65 who commit suicide
4,010	Number of suicides, ages 15–25
790,000	Estimated number of suicide attempts per year
3	Female attempts for each male attempt
5,000,000	Number of Americans who have attempted suicide
6	Number of individuals intimately affected by a given suicide
264	Number of suicides in 2002 by individuals under age 15
1	Rank of Wyoming in suicides per 100,000 residents
6,246	Number of females who committed suicide in 2002
65+	Age group in which suicide is most common[7]
1,939	Number of African Americans who committed suicide in 2002
17,108	Number of completed suicides involving firearms[8]
42	Percentage of gay/lesbian youth who sometimes or often think of suicide[9]
33	Percentage gay/lesbian youth who reported at least one attempt at suicide[10]
4	Percentage of adolescents who reported at least one suicide attempt in past year[11]
3	Rank of suicide as cause of death among adolescents[12]
60	Percentage of adolescents who have a friend who has attempted suicide[13]
20	Percentage of adolescents who have a friend who has attempted suicide *in past year*[14]
1,000	Number of suicides on university campuses each year[15]

9.5   Percentage of college students who seriously considered suicide[16]

1.5   Percentage of college students who have made a suicide attempt[17]

40   Percentage rate of suicide by male physicians higher than other males[18]

90   Percentage of people who are mentally ill at time of suicide[19]

60   Percentage of suicides using firearms[20]

80   Percentage of firearm suicides by males[21]

86   Percentage of survivors in one study who report feeling guilty[22]

25   Percentage of all persons who are drunk when they committed suicide[23]

10   Percentage of fatal shootings by police officers provoked by people actively seeking to die[24]

As these statistics suggest, suicide is not so rare as we might think. We must ask ourselves, if we were willing to speak more openly about suicide's proximity to our lives, might we be able to do something to prevent the deaths of so many?

Perspectives on the Statistics

From God's perspective, one suicide death is too many. Jesus' parable of the one lost sheep, in which a shepherd searches ceaselessly for the one sheep lost from a fold of ninety-nine, supports that conclusion (Luke 15:4–7). In an individualistic age, however, some counter that if an individual wants to end his life, he has that right. Many who idolize individualism would agree with former Supreme Court Justice Sandra Day O'Connor, who wrote in a judicial opinion, "At the heart of liberty is the right to define one's own concept of existence, of meaning, of the universe, and of the mystery of human life."[25]

Famed poet and cleric John Donne, who had considered suicide himself, argued that suicide ought to be humanly understandable and forgivable by God. In *Biathanatos*, published fifteen years after his natural death, Donne wrote, "Whensoever any affliction assails me, methinks I have the keys of my prison in mine own hand, and no remedy presents itself so soon to my heart as mine own sword."[26] Yet Donne did not suicide, and Alan Alvarez, in *The Savage God*, suggests that writing *Biathanatos* became an alternative to suicide for him.

> He set out to find precedents and reasons for killing himself while still remaining Christian—or, at least, without damning himself eternally. But the process of writing the book and marshaling his intricate learning and dialectical skill may have relieved the tension and helped to re-establish his sense of his self.[27]

Donne shows us that there are many ways to think about suicide, and also that there are a variety of ways to deal with the thoughts of suicide that come to so many of us. The options that intellectuals and theologians like Justice O'Connor and John Donne offer us can help us think more empathetically about those who have struggled with, and even chosen to follow, suicidal thoughts.

Yet some survivors see the issue differently, from a perspective that is equally as important and decidedly urgent. "Why, as a society, are we choosing not to make [suicide prevention] a priority?" demands Mark Chafee, president of the Suicide Prevention Advocacy Network (SPAN). Chafee's 16-year-old son, Eric, suicided.[28] When we review the statistics compiled on suicide, how can Americans remain untroubled with a growing phenomenon that leaves so many survivors with hearts sore with grief? Whatever each person's rights, don't we want to offer help to those considering suicide but still living? And what of those struggling to live in suicide's wake?

From Numbers to Stories

In a culture that crunches numbers, prizes statistics, turns phenomena into spreadsheets and graphs, PowerPoint presentations, journal articles, government reports and documents, suicide is reduced to digits, percentages, rankings, trends. This culture overlooks *people*, the survivors whose worlds have been radically altered without their permission.

Each suicide is a human being with a face, a voice, a laugh. An unrepeatable, unique gift of God. What happened to their dreams, hopes, longings, ambitions, stories? What happened to their belongings, junk, secrets? What happens to that portion of the world they were to love, to influence, to repair?

Each suicide creates stories. Sometimes a family's stories clash with and contradict each other, depending on the teller. Some family members will not allow certain facts to penetrate their versions of the story. They enlist only facts that make them comfortable. Holly Nelson-Becker, of the University of Kansas, identifies four kinds of narratives that can apply to the stories of survivors of suicides:

+ the past original and reconsidered event
+ the present retold narrative
+ the current perspective of the storyteller
+ the perception of the story the listener may want to hear.[29]

I would add a fifth: a narrative written by God, a "next chapter" for the deceased and for the survivor.

Stories are subject to being revisited and reinterpreted. In writing this book, I have revisited the narrative of my cousin's suicide in 1974. In a desire to make meaning of the death, through recent questions and conversations, I have gained new details and insights to blend into the narrative. In some ways, it has been like a cone inserted into a kettle of cotton candy. The cone represents the basic details: Wilma suicided. But the retellings of the narrative added more substance, like rotations around the kettle rim.

Each suicide has survivors. The American Association of Suicidology, in 2004, estimated that six individuals intimately affected by the loss survive every suicide.[30] Adina Wrobleski places the number at ten.[31] Crosby and Nash suggest that 7 percent of the population has been affected by suicide.[32] Each suicide comes from a unique person with a story of their own, and their choice to die touches numerous other storylines, those of the people who continue to live in relationship to them.

An Enduring Effect

No suicide is an isolated social or spiritual experience. Any suicide creates a wake of consequences that touch a lot of shoreline in current and future generations. The silence that often conceals suicide in shame does not prevent the death from affecting those who survive it. Many family history buffs have been stunned to discover—or uncover—how Uncle Roy or Grandma Allen really died, and the recognition of how much that new truth explains about a family's dynamics can be equally astonishing. Thirty-seven years passed before the death of Kermit Roosevelt, in 1943, was acknowledged by family members as suicide rather than a heart attack.[33]

Even when it is acknowledged, a suicide powerfully affects those in its sphere. Iris Bolton captured the initial experience following her son's suicide:

> A suicide in a house is a surprise package. It is a bomb tossed through a transom, that rips your door off the hinges and admits an army of invaders including newspaper reporters, the curious, the sensation seekers, cemetery salesmen, undertakers, and tombstone promoters.[34]

Suicide is the long shadow that falls across family narratives, oblivious to all attempts to sanitize facts and circumstances and to forget. In some families, suicide is the snoring elephant in the room. Joshua Logan, movie producer, describes the barriers he confronted:

> I couldn't ask questions about my dead father without people coughing or changing the subject.
> "Quiet," they would say, "here comes Josh Junior." They always acted so funny and secretly that I finally stopped asking

questions about my daddy. How could I know it was going to take forty years . . . for me to learn some gruesome and tragic facts about his death, and see him clearly then for the first time in my life?[35]

Peter Selwyn's father suicided when Peter was 18 months old. The AIDS specialist at Yale has spent years updating and filling in gaps in the narrative. He described the obstacles placed in the way of his curiosity:

> As a child, whenever I asked, which was not very often, I was told that he had died in a fall from a window, that he had had poor balance, and that this was a terrible accident. I suppose that this seemed so bizarre that maybe I believed it was true; or else, given the way people's expressions and tones of voice would change whenever I brought it up, I got the message that this was not something that was acceptable to discuss. My mother would use an awkward, slightly disapproving tone when she used the phrase "your father," which is the only way that I have ever heard her refer to him.[36]

So resolute was the family silence, Selwyn came to doubt his father's existence. Decades later, after a Christmas concert at the Cathedral of Saint John the Divine in Manhattan, he paused to notice memorial candles representing those who had died of AIDS. Selwyn began to cry at the thought of how many of his patients had died. "I was confronted with the deaths of all these young men and women whom I could no more save than I could have saved my father," Selwyn writes. In that moment, he started to understand that he "had never come to terms with this first and primal loss."[37]

He concluded that the effort to know the truth, although emotionally demanding, "saved my life, or . . . at the very least it enabled me to give up a burden that I had carried for almost thirty-five years without even having been aware of its presence."[38]

As Jann Fielden noted, "For family members left behind, the suffering, the wondering, the pain of bereaving remain, sometimes for the rest of their lives."[39] In Selwyn's case, the silence led to family estrangement. Decades later, Selwyn has begun to reconnect with his father's family, abandoned for years like the memories of his father.

Survivors may chase the desire to escape the suicide of a loved one, to pretend that it never happened or that it does not leave a lasting mark. But talk about closure, "moving on," and "getting over it" is easier verbalized than experienced. Ryan, a survivor, captures the indelible reality of a suicide:

> You can clean up the room. You can dispose of their stuff. You can have a funeral. You can settle their estate. You can talk about "moving on" with your own life. But the suicide remains. My father ended his life far short of the "threescore and ten" and long before his children's need for a father ended. He is an unseen guest at every family gathering, every wedding, every baptism of a newborn. He is the dating point: an event happened *before* or *after* his suicide.

What Is Lost

After doing the research for this book, after listening to the narratives of survivors who have intersected my work as a thanatologist, after looking at the pictures of their loved ones, I am haunted by the fact that they who suicided, generally, died alone. Not just physically alone but, in many cases, emotionally and spiritually alone. My mind keeps going back to the adolescent, sitting alone on a dock at a lake near the family's mountain cabin, unable to take in the beauty of that place as he wrapped weights to his body with duct tape. Weights to carry him to the bottom. A descent, he hoped, that would end his aloneness and would silence the accusations about him. He had lain naked in another adolescent male's arms and experienced a reality he could not ignore and his family could never accept. It was only a matter of time until family members found out that he was not like them, not the way they wanted him to be, not like the script of "wholesomeness" and family values they mandated for their polished public image. The dissonance between the expectation of disappointing his family and the memories of shared awakening and ecstasy had dragged him to this precipice of despair. If only he could have talked to someone, but in his religious circles it had become evident that no compassion would be found. He had heard his own dad snarl about homosexuals, "They ought to cut their nuts off." The boy could not garner enough courage to imagine a future. He died in the stark absence of hope on his emotional horizon.

What might this boy have become? What repairs would he have made to some dimension of the flawed universe? What joy might he have brought to a lifetime partner? How might God have used his life? He became, as some calloused individuals maintain, one in 31,655, statistically insignificant in a world of 6.5 billion humans.

We may question if very many suicides wanted to *die*—or to die that day, that night. They wanted the pain, the accusations, the shame, the threats to be over, the voices to be silenced. But those feelings, and those realities, do not appear in a list of statistics. It is common to hear the assessment, "He took his life." Increasingly, by listening closely to the stories survivors tell about those who have died, I have come to believe the phrase "his life took him" is sometimes more accurate.

You, perhaps, are reading this book because, like me, you are one of the six (or sixteen or sixty) individuals who have been affected by a particular suicide. You got the call in the middle of the night, in the middle of a meal, or in the middle of a busy workday. Finding the body or being notified of a death changed suicide from an abstract idea, a list of numbers, into a grueling reality. In the words of Kay Redfield Jamison, a suicide attempter *and* a psychiatrist, you may live with "the hole in the heart that is such a terrible thing."[40]

You sat on the front row at a funeral or memorial service. You rode in a quiet limousine following a hearse. You may have written the check, or offered the credit card, that paid for the funeral care.

You have sifted through papers, possessions, clothes, photographs, deciding what to keep, what to give away, what to sell at a yard sale, what to throw away.

You have sat staring into space by the hour hoping for an answer to find you.

You have lain nakedly alone in a bed you once shared.

You have turned away from a lover's initiating touch.

You have experienced the haunting stillness of a residence touched by suicide.

You have asked, "Why?" until, not just your voice is hoarse, but your soul is hoarse.

You have lain on a couch too exhausted to move.

You have stared at a plate of food, or moved morsels of food around on a plate.

You cannot remember a conversation that just took place. You cannot focus on simple tasks.

You have stared out a windshield and wondered, "How did I get here?"

You have moaned, screamed, ranted, "I cannot survive this!"

You, perhaps, have toyed with the idea of joining the deceased one.

The Hard Work of Surviving

I believe that the hardest psychological and spiritual work humans do is surviving a suicide. The next hardest work is sharing what we are learning. Comedian Joan Rivers embraced three goals after the suicide of her husband Edgar: "I needed to know exactly what had happened; why it had happened; and what it had meant."[41] Surviving *this* particular suicide is especially difficult when it is

+ an individual you brought into this world.
+ the individual who brought you into this world.
+ an individual who promised to love you forever.
+ an individual who promised to be there for you "for always."
+ an individual who once turned your loins into an inferno.

+ an individual who whispered, "Come grow old with me. . . ."
+ an individual who gave your life meaning.

From friendships to faith, suicide changes everything. Survivors must negotiate the altered landscape of relationships, and no relationship is immune to the effect of this death. Conversations can be laced with glances that warn, "No trespassing." Some survivors are not sure what they believe anymore. Or what they can believe: God? Heaven? Grace? Prayer? Hell? Angels? All the familiar spiritual comforters are challenged by suicide, just as bridges and high-rises in California are challenged by earthquakes, and must be checked for damage immediately after one occurs.

Most especially, our connection to the one who has died suffers unexpected changes. We may find ourselves amazed when we speak words of disbelief:

"I never thought he would go through with it . . ."
"I never thought it would happen in our family . . . to me . . . to us."
"There must have been something more that I could have done, or said, or been, or given, or . . ."

As we second-guess ourselves, we may find ourselves questioning how well we even knew the one who has died. In some cases, there were elements in the deceased's life that were unknown to us. Now we ask, "Who *was* this person?"

The Christian gospel outrageously teeters on an unbelievable Easter moment in which Jesus was raised from the dead, and which connects to a future moment when we—and all those we have loved—will be raised, too, from the dead. It demands a response to an invitation to believe the unbelievable: that nothing we do as humans is the last word, and that the last word about any human being is always God's word. No suicide is the last line on anyone's spiritual vita. As Bishop C. Fitzsimmons Allison stated in his funeral homily for General William C. Westmoreland: "When we believe that there is no resurrection every criticism, every ingratitude, every failure threatens to be seen as the last word. Bitterness and despair is the fruit of a world-limited hope."[42]

But if we believe in resurrection—even if we invest in it with fingers crossed—we leave those we love open to God's gifted mercy. When we believe in the resurrection, we are free to remember the life rather than the details of the death.

In 1995, Bishop David Johnson, the Episcopal Bishop of the Diocese of Massachusetts, ended his life with a gunshot. How could one who so zealously preached resurrection—who could make it believable—commit, in his own darkness, suicide? That act on a cold January day in 1995 is not, however, the last word about David Johnson. Bishop-coadjutor M. Thomas Shaw, SSJE, his successor, preached at David's funeral:

> David, in the extremity of his leap into the dark, has leapt into the arms of Christ, into the judgment of truth, into the transforming fire of conversion. His purging, forgiveness and glorification is underway. We share in this process by praying for him, offering our love, however confused and ambivalent just now, to be used by God to bless, heal and restore him.

Then Bishop Shaw offered seventeen words packed with Easter hope that is equally true of your loved one:

> Next time we meet David he will be in his glory, a man wounded, rescued and saved.[43]

Your initial reaction and response to this suicide will not be the last word either. I hope that you will use this wounding you yourself have experienced, somehow, someway, to bless the world.

I hope that you will let the God who grieves be your companion all the days of your grief.

I hope that grace will become more precious to you.

I hope that your soul will be stretched to an outrageous love.
I hope that you will laugh again.
I hope you will be overwhelmed by your joy.
I hope that you will dance on a distant day.
Swedish immigrants to America brought a rich tradition of hymn lyrics that have birthed hope in many survivors. I cherish this promise:

Neither life nor death shall ever
From the Lord his children sever;
Unto them his grace he showeth,
And their sorrows all he knoweth.[44]

Reflection: Spend some time with the following hymn text. Underline or highlight words or phrases that resonate with you. Close your eyes and reflect on the promise of the hymn. Suicide is a "tumult of our life's wild, restless sea." Imagine the waves churning, pounding the shoreline.

Jesus calls us; o'er the tumult of our life's wild, restless sea.
day by day his clear voice soundeth, saying
"Christian, follow me."

In our joys and in our sorrows, days of toil and hours of ease,
still he calls, in cares and pleasures,
"Christian, love me more than these."[45]

Prayer: Knower of Our Sorrows, you comprehend our be-
     wilderment and pain better than we do. Nothing we do,
     or that is done to us, catches you by surprise. No one is
     ever "lost" to you. No human is a statistic to you, who sees
     the sparrow fall. You saw my loved one slip into eternity's
     embrace. Help me remember that my loved one, named by
     you, is still graced by you and even now you are working
     to bring resurrection. Help me trust that on some distant
     Easter morning, you will have the last word. Amen.

Chapter 2

Asking Why, Saying Goodbye

He left
without so much as a hint of a why
and without giving us
a chance to say goodbye.
Would he have made such a choice
had he known
how much we would grieve
in the absence of a functional why?

> In the public telling of our tales we seek help in find-
> ing answers, or at least, permission to share the burning
> questions.
> —*Robert Neimeyer*[1]

Historian Stephen Ambrose could write academically about suicide. Emory Upton, the subject of his book *Upton and the Army*, was a Civil War major general by the age of 25. He committed suicide at 42. Soon after Ambrose's book was published, a key point on the trail to tenure, his wife, Judy, a genius battling depression, committed suicide and left him with children aged seven and five. In those early days of surviving, could he have imagined becoming one of America's most popular writers of history, with a string of bestsellers including *D-Day, Citizen Soldiers,* and *Undaunted Courage?* Could he have imagined being military adviser on the blockbuster movie *Saving Private Ryan?* Could he have imagined someday writing poignantly about the suicide of Captain Meriwether Lewis? Could

Stephen Ambrose have imagined a future in a present littered with unanswered why's?[2]

Imagining a Future Not Dominated by "Why's"

In a present littered with why's, how comfortable are you voicing your questions? Who is open to hearing, perhaps one more time, the questions that harangue your soul? Who has stopped listening to you?

"Why?" or "WHY!!!" is breathed, screamed, prayed, whispered by suicide survivors in every language. Some survivors step into the question the first thing upon awakening; for others, it will be the last thing on their mind when, and if, sleep overtakes them. Some will leave no stone unturned in seeking, weighing, constructing, and rejecting explanations.

"Why?" is too thin a word to meet all the demands and longings of survivors. Three letters create the driving question that dominates waking hours and, sometimes, dreams.

> Every why I try
> comes up short
> of the explanation I am craving—
> an explanation I can live with.

C. J. Van Dongen contends that the "agonizing questioning of suicide" crowds out other aspects of living.[3] The why's dart, like guerrillas in a war zone, at will, into worship, sexual intimacy, work, shopping, showers and shaving, and any attempts at relaxation. A thousand scents, sounds, and memory slices can trigger an avalanche of new why's.

I sometimes suggest to those who ask why, "I know what you're looking for—some definite 'there' answer that ends the questioning—but what answer will you *settle* for?" Some survivors get a preliminary "why" in a note left by the one who has died. To some, the note makes sense, but not to others. Some survivors hope that someone can translate the rambling of the note into an understandable language. Some decipher the words with all the intensity of a wartime code breaker. Some seek the "clues" that will unlock the triumvirate of riddles: "Why? Why *now*? Why *this* way?"

Sometimes survivors are denied access to the note. Someone may have taken it upon themselves to decide it was too brutal, too accusatory, too intimidating. "It is best if she/he not see this," such actions seem to say. That decision may, in some cases, be wise if the suicide used the note to inflict a final insult or implant blame. Nevertheless, Alison Wertheimer notes, "Having a note which makes it clear that the victim intended to die can help survivors accept the reality of the death" and limit the lingering sting of why's.[4] When withheld, an important clue for integration of the loss is sometimes denied those who need it most.

In the psychological literature on suicide the estimates of note-leavers vary from 15 to 25 percent of all who take their own lives. Edwin Shneidman, after studying thousands of suicide notes, cautions that notes do not offer easy explanations of why someone has committed suicide, although they appear to provide special insights into the death. While notes may produce some information, Wertheimer suggests that notes produce variable responses and "can affect the survivor's reactions to the death" depending on how the survivor(s) interprets the note.[5] Carol Staudacher concludes:

> It is important to put the note into perspective. That is, it is one item which reflects your loved one's thinking along a whole continuum of thought. The note is not necessarily representational of the same mind which conceived the suicide and carried it out. The note only represents your loved one's state of mind when the note was written. *It is a mistake to try to extract the essence of the tragedy from this one piece of communication. . . .* [italics mine][6]

Vince Foster, deputy White House Counsel early in the Clinton Administration, was found dead of an apparently self-inflicted gunshot wound on the evening of July 20, 1993. Foster's note, found torn into pieces in his briefcase, was accusatory: "I was not meant for the job in the spotlight in Washington. Here ruining people is considered sport. . . ."[7] Few suicide notes have been the object of such speculation and attention, ricocheting through the canyons of political power and influence. Long after Foster's death, pundits and researchers argued over the exact meaning of the note.

On the other hand, some notes relieve survivors of responsibility. When survivors are left clueless—with no note—they try out answers like a shopper trying on clothes at a bargain sale. They have an insatiable hunger for a reason.

Jack Jordan offers one significant "answer" to the question why that has helped many survivors. He calls it "the perfect storm." As hurricanes form in the Gulf of Mexico, numerous factors interact to create a level 3, 4, or 5 storm—all of the elements that could create a storm of immense power suddenly converge. Jordan sees this as a potential metaphor for some suicides. He contends that a particular suicide may have happened because of "a whole host of facts in just the right combination."[8]

Jackson uses the graphic of a large cluster of interlinking circles to depict his idea. Among these circles, which represent factors in the death, are genetics, substance abuse, personality, impulsiveness, past experiences with suicide attempts, life stresses, social issues, lack of communication, hopelessness, access to means such as guns or poison, and so on.[9] The interaction of these factors may lead to a particular breaking point, a decision that leads to suicide at 7:30 on a Monday evening in October.

Ultimately, knowing the reasons someone chose to end their life will probably always evade us. But our unknowing does not have to end in total despair. I love a Southern folk hymn, "We will understand it better, by and by." According to the logic of the song, we will live our way into understanding in a "by and by"—if not in this world, then in the next.

Levels of Why

I believe that there are three levels of why's: initial, transitional, and transformative. If a survivor will not settle for the first explanation that "comes down the pike," there is hope, in time, of a fuller explanation.

Initial Why's

In the early moments following a suicide, someone may step forward with an answer that survivors seize for lack of a better explanation. Some survivors grasp this initial response the way a drowning individual clings to a life preserver. However, this response is probably more a *why* response than a well-considered explanation of what has happened. There are no flawless answers, especially immediately after a death. In some cases, these are merely attempts to be kind. Would-be comforters do not know what else to say.

You may never get answers to what happened, but you will get responses passed off as answers. Admittedly, at some point, these kinds of initial answers must often be abandoned as inadequate. But if they get you out of the threatening current, closer to shore where you can stand, they may prove useful.

Transitional Why's

When the fact of this suicide settles in and becomes part of the fabric of life, survivors refine their why responses. This process can take time, and it requires concentrated consideration. Transitional why responses are like rough drafts. Take this book as an example. You are not reading the first draft of this book. Under the eyes and hearts of skilled editors, I reworked sentences and paragraphs many times over, searching for the right version of my thoughts. The finished product is a far different work than the initial draft. Why responses to a suicide change in a similar way.

Sociologist Tony Walter writes of the need for mediators to respond to our why's.

> One of the things that mourners do is search for a story about the deceased's life that makes sense to them and that, ideally, can be shared with others. . . . If the public, publicized, story is acceptable, then this validates the deceased's life and its meaning to the mourner. But if the public story is unacceptable, incorrect or misleading, then mourning becomes complicated by the drive to set the public record straight, or is compounded by extra grief over a last public statement that cannot be corrected.[10]

We expect why's will be addressed, or at least acknowledged, in funerals or memorial services.

> For many people the funeral tribute is the only occasion at which the meaning of a person's life is publicly stated, so it is a terrible indictment on the celebrant if mourners feel s/he failed to capture the essence of the person.[11]

Many do not want the last line of the person's résumé to read: suicide. Bill Clinton, in his memoir, revisited Vince Foster's suicide and wrote another line in the life of his colleague.

> Vince was overwhelmed, exhausted, and vulnerable to attacks by people who didn't play by the same rules he did. He was rooted in the values of honor and respect, and uprooted by those who valued power and personal assault more. And his untreated depression stripped him of the defenses that allowed the rest of us to survive.[12]

Jack Jordan, who has done extensive work with suicide survivors, points to "an intense need to create an explanatory narrative."[13] As a survivor, you will be blessed—if you decide to be—by "editors" or mediators who will come into your grief and ask you to reframe some of your thoughts and storyline, however cherished. It may be a book, a sermon, a comment overheard on an airplane or in a restaurant that leads you to reexamine an explanation. "Editors" appear in unlikely places, on unlikely occasions, and in the most unlikely voices. Some may anger you. Others will serve like a kiln bringing out the beauty of the glaze of an answer.

In a small pottery shop in San Miguel, Mexico, while writing this manuscript, I found a beautiful statue of a peasant woman. (To be honest, the 50 percent off sign first attracted my eye.) At that price how could I *not* buy it? As I looked closely, I realized the glaze was not uniform. Gaps distracted from the character of the pottery. Although the imperfection was hardly noticeable, I had seen it. I would continue to "see" the blemish after I purchased it. I placed the pottery back on the shelf and mumbled, "I need to think about it. . . ."

Well-meaning individuals will offer you "50 percent off" responses. Examine gifted why-explanations thoughtfully. If you notice a flaw in the glaze, pay attention. You will learn to decipher the counterfeit in time. Easy answers do not soothe a survivor's heart.

On the other hand, you must be open, in the transitioning, to a fragment of a response being helpful. That fragment may be the grain of sand trapped in the oyster that becomes the pearl, comfort in the dark moments.

Transformative Why's

The third response is the lived-with response. It percolates over time to transform us. I have met survivors who remain trapped emotionally and spiritually by suicide. They have never reached the stage of transformation, in a spiritual sense, that may evolve from their loss. Some become martyrs. "You know her daughter killed herself"—the whispered explanation of a wasted life. Louise DeSalvo writes about her mother,

In the years that have intervened since my sister's death, my mother's pain is clearly visible, ever present. She stops enjoying my children. She stops enjoying our family gatherings. She stops enjoying everything. Her mouth is permanently drawn downward into a frown. When we take family pictures, she forces a smile. She pushes herself, each day, through her routine, through her life. She isn't with us. She's with Jill.[14]

What is true of DeSalvo's mother is true of many "survivors":

Since my sister's suicide, my mother had drifted further and further away from us into the underworld of memory. When my sister killed herself, she took my mother with her to keep her company.[15]

Some survivors refuse to accept "getting over it" as a spiritual goal. They do not resonate with "getting beyond this" or "moving on with life." Rather, for the courageous, the goal becomes to move *into* the maelstrom, the chaos, like a plane flying into the eye of a hurricane. They ask the Genesis question, "Can order come from this chaos?" Some survivors, with the perseverance of Jacob wrestling with the angel, mumble or declare, "I will not let go unless you bless me" (Genesis 32:26). Or they persevere until their experience of surviving a suicide empowers them to bless others. Judy Collins, years after the suicide of her son Clark, explained: "Without the wound there is no miracle. And I know these wounds are the entrance to a power greater than I am—an entrance to God, and, once more, to grace. Without it I am doomed."[16] Collins could not have written those words immediately after Clark's death. It took time for the reality to be formed on the forge of her heart and to emerge into her consciousness. It took time to rehearse the why's.

Nan Zastrow, following her 19-year-old son's suicide, could have drawn up the bridge over the moat, climbed to the tower and waited for her own death. Rather, she chose to create a newsletter that has blessed countless numbers of grievers and caregivers. No little sugar-coated nuggets of comfort from Nan. Some of her words annoy individuals who wanted her to "move on":

> Acquaintances and friends avoided the subject of Chad's death as though I was afflicted with a contagious disease. Did they think by associating with me this could happen to them too? I felt alone in my pain.[17]

Nan's experience shows that reaching the stage of the "transformative why" does not come with the promise of comfort.

The transformative why may also imbue the survivor with responsibility: In the living room of a stunning high-rise condominium, sobbing punctuated the stillness like thunder on a July night. Trinkets of success filled the space; the address itself signaled that this family had "arrived." Unpleasant things did not happen to this family, or at least they could be "dealt with." The couple, who earned six-figure incomes by solving problems for corporations and governments, had long lived by the adage: "We can deal with anything that happens." There had been moments in their son's life when the adage had been tested and strengthened. Now, one bullet shattered the accouterments of comfort and security they had accumulated.

Friends came. Would-be comforters crossed the room to the couple huddled on the couch; friends, in small groups around the margins of the room, fumbled with thoughts. The visitors had gathered here before on social occasions and parties and celebrations, but never for a wake. Some looked away, never having seen the couple not "in control." The words of visitors with reputations as wordsmiths, clinicians, and pulpiteers disintegrated before reaching the shores of the couple's distress.

Now another couple arrived, fearing they were intruding. The grieving father looked up, saw the face of another man, and thought, "Finally, someone who understands."

Three years before, that man and his wife had sat, head in hands, moaning, devastated by the discovery of their own son's suicide. This new survivor had arrived on their doorstep with well-rehearsed proclamations of the goodness and faithfulness of God. "God has his ways we do not always understand. It is not for us to ask why."

Now, these two fathers moved toward the middle of the living room and embraced with bear-like intensity. The veteran whispered simply, "I know. I *know*."

In that place and moment, the Holy Spirit worked through a broken father who had lived with unresolved why's following his son's suicide until the experience *transformed* him. He came bearing not answers but wounds. "Been there, felt that, wondered that. . . ." His 22-year-old's suicide had become the equivalent of Saul's Damascus Road experience. Upon hearing the recent news, he had told his wife, "We have to go. They will need us. The bullshitters are already there trying to dowse their grief."

For many, suicide is a blinding light that forces us to see our most entrenched assumptions differently.

A World That Wants Answers

Survivors grieve answerless in a world that wants answers. Now. Why's drive survivors on all kinds of emotional and spiritual journeys. Some to libraries and bookstores to sample the experience of others, some to clinicians, some to circles of fellow survivors, some to practitioners of New Age thinking, some to their communities of faith, or to new communities of faith when the familiar spiritual well comes up dry, some to circles of the deceased's friends. Looking, always looking, for a clue that has resisted discovery.

Expect Someone to Short-Circuit Your Why's

Individuals who nominate themselves to be God's field reps in a crisis squelch questions in order to protect God's reputation and drive the hard questions underground. I often share this enfranchising quote from baseball great Dave Dravecky, whose pitching career ended when his arm was amputated.

There is no such thing as a bad question. The issue is not with the questions, or even how we ask them. The issue is where we go with questions. Any question that brings us to God for an answer is a good question.[18]

The great tragedy in suicide is not the unanswered or unanswerable questions but the disenfranchised questions. "You'll drive yourself nuts if you keep asking these questions," Herb was told after his wife's suicide. Some days Herb thought he had already gone nuts.

Living in a World Without Answers

Can you live with a world without good answers to your why's?

Can you live with a God who will not interrupt your why's with anything that resembles an answer?

Can you survive the incessant cheap answers that will be offered by well-intended but badly informed friends and acquaintances?

Mainstream Christianity has missed out on so many tools for grievers by relying on an overly intellectual approach. Many mainline Christians have never heard a decent rendition of "Precious Lord, Take My Hand." When Mahalia Jackson sang it at Martin Luther King's funeral, neither she nor those in attendance were in any hurry for her to dash through the lyrics. Broken, she sang as if she had forever to finish. "Through the storm, through the night," was punctuated by fervent *Yes, Lord*'s from across the grieving congregation. "Lead me on, to the light, precious Lord, take my hand, lead me home."[19]

God never snaps impatiently, "Listen up! I am only going to explain this one more time!" God understands our inability to understand and that we must live our ways into a why.

Ask your why's—every last one of them—until you are hoarse. Do not let anyone take away your why's. Your why's are as much a part of you as your DNA. Your persistence in voicing why will eventually benefit you, and possibly others. As the great Roman poet Ovid once observed, "Welcome this pain, for some day it will be useful to you."

When the moment comes, as it most likely will, that you can dance despite an anguished heart strewn with why's, doubters will remember your persistence in asking why's.

Victor Parachin insists that there is nothing wrong with asking why. Why is a normal response to life's unexplainable outrageous untimely experiences. Parachin counters that the *better* question is "Now what?" *Now what* do I do with my loved one's suicide? Ask God, "Now what?" and you will get a response.

My friend Greg Adams attends a church in which the "children's sermon" is an element of Sunday worship. The minister once told Greg, "Seeing your daughter walking down the aisle for 'children's time' strikes fear in my heart." One Sunday, the pastor sought to convey the idea that God is like a mother hen. Laura replied, "God is like a chicken? That sure doesn't make any sense to me."

I wish more survivors verbalized their dissonance: "That sure doesn't make any sense to me." I almost believe that a person responding, "That is the dumbest explanation I have ever heard!" would do answer-bearers a world of good.

I hope there is a station called "Answers" during orientation in eternity, where new arrivals exchange mysteries and wonderings, puzzlements and why's for celestial-calibrated answers. So that new arrivals step into heaven's splendor shed of the last hurdle to a "good time."

Instead of answers, perhaps we will get reunions with our beloved, and, in some cases, not so beloved, dead. The Gospels depict Jesus healing the "demon-possessed" man, who had "broken his chains and had been driven . . . into solitary places." Many suicide survivors feel that they have been "driven" to solitary places by others' reactions to their why's. But when the people "came to Jesus, they found the man from whom the demons had gone out, sitting at Jesus' feet, dressed and in his right mind" (Luke 8:35). The story offers prophetic hope that kindles anticipation within us. I believe when some come to Jesus through death, we will hear, "There is someone I want you to see. . . ." In eternity's day, survivors will erupt with joy as they abandon the chains of their why's. I love the promise in the hymn "God be with you 'til we meet again":

'Til we meet, 'til we meet.
'Til we meet at Jesus' feet.

Sometimes as I sing that song I stop, overwhelmed by the longing in my heart for the words to be fulfilled. I have a deep longing, that in those first moments experiencing eternity's reality, I will rediscover my cousin Wilma, "dressed and in her right mind" with all the shackles gone that prevented a "full meaningful life" for her. I will know her as I never was able to know her in her psychological distress and spiritual darkness. The Book of Common Prayer poses the question "Why do we pray for the dead?" It answers, "We pray for them, because we still hold them in our love, and because we trust that in God's presence those who have chosen to serve him will grow in his love, until they see him as he is."[20]

In God's presence, all barriers to fully experiencing his grace, and all barriers to being transformed, will end. Many, like Wilma, will at last realize how deeply they have been loved by God through the ups and downs of psychological turmoil. For that reason, the canyons of heaven will continuously resound with sounds of celebration and laughter.

There, survivors will finally be able to abandon threadbare why's. In the meantime, however, we do well to accept the permission, offered by Rainer Maria Rilke, to ask and live and love the questions:

... be patient toward all that is unresolved in your heart and try to love the *questions themselves* like locked rooms and like books that are written in a very foreign tongue. Do not now seek the answers, which cannot be given you because you would not be able to live them. And the point is, to live everything. *Live* the questions now. Perhaps you will then gradually, without noticing it, live along some distant day into the answer.[21]

I will go to my grave with why's frayed around the edges. But they co-exist with the suggestion passed down from the wisdom of Benedict in the sixth century, "And never lose hope in God's mercy."[22]

The spiritual task of survivors is living with why's.

Reflection: Spend some moments with the following reflection:

> Most days I am like the world's most determined
> jigsaw puzzle champion pressing on
> although others have abandoned this puzzle,
> determined that I will assemble
> the puzzle that has remained so long in pieces.
> I tell myself that it's only a matter of time
> until the critical "Aha!" wanders into my mind
> and, at last, I will know
> what made him do it.
> Then, I remind myself
> that he will still be just as dead,
> just as gone.

Prayer: Fountain of Mercy, our why's do not exasperate you.
In our inability to understand tragedy, you form us, deepen
our hearts, and heighten our anticipation of your kingdom.
Give us, as survivors, the courage to resist easy answers
that require little of us. Remind us that, in your grace, we
will live our way into that distant moment when why's will
have answers. Amen.

Chapter 3

Permitting Ourselves
to Grieve and Survive

So many times, I signed
permission slips for school field trips.
She would come home insisting
that we listen to her vivid descriptions
of what she had seen, heard, experienced.
She never asked permission for this trip.

> [Grief following a suicide] is a personal process: idiosyncratic, intimate, and inextricable from our sense of who we are.
>
> —*Robert Neimeyer*[1]

Kermit, son of Theodore and Edith Roosevelt, tried to live up to his father's sense of adventure. He accompanied his father on an African safari before beginning his studies at Harvard. Kermit was part of the ill-fated expedition on the River of Doubt in Brazil, when his father pondered ending his life so as not to slow down the party, which was short of food. Impatient to fight in World War I, Kermit joined the British forces before the U.S. entered the war. Between wars, he founded the Roosevelt Steamship Company and United States Lines. He again served with British forces before Pearl Harbor. After the Roosevelt family secured an Army commission for him, through cousin Franklin, Kermit served at Fort Richardson, Alaska. But his alcoholism severely limited opportunities for combat duty and muddied the

43

Roosevelt reputation. On June 4, 1953, "Unable to bear the life of inaction to which he was condemned, unable to tame the demons which plagued him,"[2] Roosevelt put his 45-caliber revolver to his chin and ended his pain.[3]

Mrs. Roosevelt went to her grave grieving the deaths of three sons on military duty (Quentin had died after being shot down over France in World War I; General Theodore Jr., part of the first wave of American soldiers in D-Day, died after a heart attack). The 82-year-old grieving mother wrote her niece, Eleanor Roosevelt: "In these days all we can do is brace ourselves to meet whatever comes. Kermit would not have shirked . . . and I who loved him so dearly must be strong to meet whatever the future brings."[4]

The Suicide Bomb

I think Edith Roosevelt would have agreed with John Hewitt's assessment, "When the suicide bomb drops . . . one group of people is always standing at ground zero: the members of the surviving family," and, I would add, close friends.[5]

In many families there may be an initial viewer, or viewers, who discovered the body, which is particularly disconcerting when there is significant trauma or decomposition.

> How long before the discovery
> begins to fade like a worn photo or jeans?
> Will I ever forget those first unbearable moments
> finding a him that no longer resembled him?
> Any good memory is silenced, superimposed
> with that forever ugly moment of discovery and shock.
> I know how citizens must feel
> in a land occupied by foreign troops.

Publisher Katharine Graham described the experience of finding her husband's body after he had shot himself:

It was so profoundly shocking and traumatizing—he was so obviously dead and the wounds were so ghastly to look at—that I just ran into the next room and buried my head in my hands, trying to absorb that this had really happened, this dreadful thing that had hung over us for the last six years. . . . The sight was so appalling that I knew I couldn't go back in, so I ran to call Buck and our caretaker, William Smith, for help.[6]

Facing Suicide in Families

Some survivors will not acknowledge the death as suicide. Sherwin Nuland, author of *How We Die*, acknowledges that only the deaths that can with some degree of certainty "be attributed to self-destruction" are part of the 30,000-plus annual suicide tally because the "stigma that still attaches to suicide is sufficient that families, and the subjects themselves, will often disguise the circumstances. Survivors sometimes appeal to a sympathetic physician to write something else on a death certificate."[7]

Within survivor families, some know the details, some know *some* of the details, and some know few, or none, of the details. Some may be deliberately kept in the dark. Jodie Johnson gave permission for her family's grief following her husband's suicide by calling a family meeting the night before the funeral service. "There will be no secrets in this family," she told them. Though some disclosures were uncomfortable to hear, the gathering, with a priest present, went a long way toward integration of the loss.[8]

Sons and daughters whose parents committed suicide seem to have an increased incidence of suicide themselves. Novelist Ernest Hemingway committed suicide in 1961; his father, Clarence, in 1928; his sister Ursula, in 1966; his brother, Leicester, in 1982 (and Leicester suspected that their sister, Marcelline, had committed suicide in 1963 notwithstanding the physician's declaration of natural causes), and his granddaughter Margaux, in 1996.[9] Among Theodore Roosevelt's descendants, his son Kermit, grandson Dirck, and granddaughter Paulina all committed suicide. Although suicide is not genetic, suicide ideation becomes embedded in the fabric and narrative of some families. Kay Redfield Jamison asks,

> Is an increased tendency to commit suicide due only to the passing on of the genetic predispositions to the psychiatric conditions most intimately linked to suicide—depression, manic depression, schizophrenia, alcoholism—all of which, especially the mood disorders have a strong genetic basis?[10]

Although no "suicide gene" exists, the occurrence of multiple suicides in some family narratives is troubling.

Permission to Grieve

Wise survivors give themselves generous permission to survive. Some choose the path of victim: "Poor me." "Look what he/she did to *me/us!*" Others take the approach of Jodie Johnson, who declared, "I will design my life."[11] She gave herself permission to imagine a new future rather than the future she had assumed she would share with her husband. Others ponder a future that might have been.

> All those boys, young men
> who played basketball in my driveway
> and plundered my refrigerator
> are now graying, balding.
> I look at them wondering
> what my son would have looked like
> the other side of forty.
> Some never know what to say to me.
> None say his name.
> Had one of those boys—rather than he—
>   have chosen such a death,
> what would my son
> have said, years later,
> to a still-grieving mom?

Some survivors join support groups as a way of giving permission to grieve. A few, after one or two sessions, drop out. One wife explained her husband's absence from meetings: "He just cannot face the honesty in the group."

Survivors have to grant themselves permission because society is reluctant to fully enfranchise their grief. Society stamps "failure" on the brows and hearts of multitudes of surviving spouses and parents. "Your child/spouse committed suicide?!" Subtle insinuations cut the suicide-ravaged heart. Having to heal the tender linings of the spirit from socially inflicted wounds only prolongs grief. Emphasizing the need for support rather than judgment, Sue Chance describes her experience:

. . . when our lives are blasted by tragedy, virtually none of us can contain all the shrapnel. Some flies out of us and hits those around us, some embeds itself near the surface and needs a little picking-at for extraction, some stays deep within us—of that, some can be gotten at with surgery and some will just have to be lived with because it's too close to a vital organ to be removed safely. We need the help of others either to take the necessary action or to bear with what we must.[12]

Survivors often sense, beneath kind words, an unspoken insinuation: If *you* had been a *better* parent/spouse/sibling/child, your loved one would never have committed suicide. If only you had done more, loved more, prayed more, cared more, taken him or her more seriously, gotten more medical attention, the individual would not have committed suicide. According to psychologists Bob Baugher and Jack Jordan, survivors have permission to limit interaction with impaired comforters and "to ask someone to make sure that certain people are *not* around you."[13]

The Individual's Choice

The individual's choice to commit suicide is compounded by the survivor(s)' choice not to grieve, or not to grieve publicly. Marilyn, a survivor of the suicide of her son, recalled,

My ex-husband demanded that all the pictures of our son be taken down. He considered Brian's suicide the ultimate act of rebellion against parental authority and the family's "good name." He kept snarling, "How could he do this to *me* after all I have done for him!" He insisted on the cheapest casket and the cheapest marker. He agreed only to a brief "family only" graveside service. Many nights as I lay in bed sobbing, he got up to go sleep in the guestroom. He went ballistic when I had "bad" days, like Brian's birthday! I finally realized I could not spend my life married to a man who would not grieve his son.

Not all spouses divorce or partners split. Some find ways to create a "suicide-free zone." "My husband and I never talk about it," one mother commented, "but I talk about Bret to the grandchildren who never got to know him. It has been 'our little secret.'"

According to urban legend, "lose a child, lose a marriage." I have read statistics suggesting that some 70 to 80 percent of parents divorce after the death of a child. However, I have found no statistical data to support these figures, and Shirley Murphy debunks such claims as injurious to parents who lose a child.[14] Some parents, however, seize the urban legend as permission to divorce. Some separate because dissonant grief-styles were "the last straw" in an unraveling relationship. Some couples simply do not have the strength or willingness to deflate the survivor's "psychache."[15]

Spirituality empowers survivors to receive spouses' wounding words. A prayer such as "Consoler, help me lovingly receive my spouse's lament. Help me respond rather than react to these troublesome words" can limit marital discord.

Some parents cannot share common grief turf. In the case of Marilyn, with a little probing, it became clear that the marriage had been troubled long before their son's suicide. Her husband continuously belittled as "pathological" her efforts to remember their son. Repeatedly he snarled, "Get over him! He's dead. Nothing you can do will change it!" This dismissal meets criteria Kenneth Doka established for "disenfranchised grief"—when individuals "incur a loss that is not or cannot be openly acknowledged, publicly mourned, or socially supported."[16] A spouse, sibling, or other family member can disenfranchise your grief. While Doka primarily identifies forces outside the marital dyad or the family, disenfranchisement internal to our most intimate relationships may challenge a family's finances and stability, particularly if the deceased was an alcoholic or a drug addict. A hinted "Your life will be better without him" can be devastating.

Marilyn decided that although there was nothing she could do about the suicide or her husband's negativity, there were things she could do *with* it. She joined a support group for parents and reached out to other surviving parents in the community. She read everything she could find on suicide. She requested her local library to buy more books on suicide. Marilyn did not "move on" but she did "move forward."

Some readers will identify with these words:

> Along the fragile walls of my heart,
> long after midnight,
> the questions dance.
> At dawnbreak,
> I wonder how my partner
> sleeps so soundly.
> Why do why's never keep him awake?

Grief Is Intimate

In the moving biblical narrative of intimacy between David and Bathsheba after the death of their unnamed child, "David comforted his wife Bathsheba, and he went to her and lay with her" (2 Samuel 12:24), which means they had intercourse. Still, nothing undermines a survivor's sex life and relational intimacy patterns like suicide. It is taboo to talk about sexuality *after* suicide. Walk into a Borders store and ask for a book on sex *and* suicide.

When counselors, uncomfortable with grief's impact on sexual expression, offer vague suggestions about "giving it time," some partners become sexually restless. Some males only know to be tender and vulnerable through sexual intimacy. Some experience in orgasm, and its complex chemical release, temporary distraction from the wrenching soul-ache that follows a suicide. But that soul-ache soon reasserts its territorial claims.

Difficulties with intimacy occur in families that cannot talk about death *and* grief *and* sexual needs. Grief-tinted intercourse is different than joy-focused intercourse. Some couples "just have to do it," in one survivor's words, "for the sake of doing it," hoping that sexual encounters will interrupt their pain.

Survivors need to confront the reality of sex and intimacy and its relationship to their grief. How has grief impacted you sexually? Would sexual intimacy be meaningful and spiritually rejuvenating? Have you given yourself permission to ask for your sexual wishes or to say "no" to a partner's initiating behaviors? Maybe you are not ready for intercourse. Co-surviving couples need negotiating skills to acknowledge sexual desires: "Just hold me" or "I want to cuddle" may be perceived as rejection by a partner. Authentic intimacy, however, honors the desires and timing of each partner. Some surviving couples, in time, experience enhanced intimacy and, through hard psychological and spiritual work, create a stronger marriage and enhanced family relationships.

Survivor couples "drift apart." The suicide may confront them with undeniable fissures in the foundation of the marriage, some long denied or camouflaged. Karl, a middle-aged survivor, reported that his wife had long been looking for a reason to stop having sex with him. "Our daughter's suicide gave her a reason. So what am I supposed to do now?"

In some instances, the avoidance of sexual intimacy with a spouse leads to sexual behaviors with other partners. Most postmortem affairs begin with the ears and eyes. One man explains,

> I could not talk to my wife about what I was feeling. She cried all the time. And no sex! At work I met a woman whose son had died by suicide a couple of years earlier. She sent me an email, "If you ever want to talk. . . ." So, we went to lunch a few times. Okay, more than a few times. I could talk to her. She

understood. I told her things I did not know I felt. Things just
happened and kept happening. Sex with her was like an oasis
in a barren desert.

Some survivors rationalized the sex as "It's-only-sex" or an affair
with "no future." One survivor contended, "It was *just* sex. I did not
feel *anything* for the woman. It's not like it was an affair." After a suicide, however, mates may not have sufficient spiritual or emotional re-
serves to deal with an affair in addition to everything else.

Adolescent and Survivor Sexual Expression

Attention needs to be paid to grieving adolescents, particularly males,
frightened or confused by the intensity of grief, who "act out" sexually. Adolescents resent anything that makes them different than
their peers. Nothing marks an adolescent as different more than surviving suicide. Nothing changes a home environment for peers more
than a suicide, especially a suicide that occurred in the adolescent's
home. Adolescents sense the change in emotional space as well as any
heightened tensions between family members. Peers may avoid coming over or "dropping by" because they are uncomfortable in a grieving
environment. One mother asked, "Why don't our children's friends come
over anymore?" I thought she meant her deceased son's friends, but she
was referring to the friends of her daughter, Heidi. Heidi was spending
more and more time away from the home. She explained:

Mom has turned the place into a mausoleum for my brother.
She had his senior picture enlarged to 24 x 36 and placed on
an easel. She has a memorial table with his pictures in the
living room. It is too much. And she never has time to listen
to what is going on in *my* world. . . . Everything is about the
world of the dead.

For some adolescent survivors, sexual activity provides a "time
out" from the sadness, a distraction from the pain. In some instances,
intercourse "just happens"—meaning that it is unplanned. Pregnancy,

of course, is sometimes a consequence, and some families seize the pregnancy as a way to escape the work of grieving.

Memory, Integration, Renewal

Survivors who try to dodge the full impact of grief will eventually experience consequences. There are no fast-track grief strategies and no speed-grief equivalents to speed-dating. Giving oneself permission to grieve takes time and courage.

Survivors must give themselves permission to actively remember the deceased. In actively remembering, survivors not only help themselves but model self-permission to individuals who may someday need this kind of courage.

Like oxygen is to the blood, memories nurture the integration of loss. In my childhood, my mom often baked "Jiffy mix" cakes. Pour the powdery mix from the box to a bowl, add a cup of water and an egg, stir, pour the batter into a cake pan, bake, spread some icing, and you have a cake for Sunday dessert. I learned I could gain quality one-on-one time with my mother by helping her bake on Saturday afternoons. The cake disappeared "in a jiffy" on Sunday. Sometimes, for variety, I would squeeze drops of food coloring into the cake batter, then draw lines in the batter with a spatula. The "marbleized" Jiffy cake elicited "oohs and ahhs."

For special Sundays, birthdays, or Christmas, my mom and I made red velvet cake. As I stirred the chocolate batter, I ran the spatula along the sides and bottom of the bowl until the ingredients were thoroughly mixed. Then I added red food coloring that I blended into the batter until every molecule was red.

Some survivors settle for a marbleized pattern instead of thorough integration of their grief. They want grief contained, controlled, perhaps brought out only on special occasions. Healthy survivors, on the other hand, integrate a suicide into the "batter" of their lives.

Following the 2001 suicide death of Andreas, their 17-year-old son, John and Inge Wickstrom integrated their loss to the degree that they could allow their loss to be featured in Tom Hennessy's articles on suicide in the *Long Beach Press-Telegram*. I noticed this healthy assessment:

Nearly three years after their son's death, John and Inge Wickstrom have not emerged from their sorrow. They may never do so, although they have become stronger and have weathered the temporary strain the suicide placed on their relationship.

They still feel incredible pain and sadness that Andreas is no longer with them. They say they are working hard to salvage lives that are worth living. "It's a daily struggle," says Inge.[17]

Robert Wicks, in *Riding the Dragon, 10 Lessons for Inner Strength in Challenging Times*, calls for finding, or creating, "renewal zones" to protect us from the annoyances of life. Safe places "provide us with a respite, a place for inner refreshment and reappraisal, and a chance to have some good old-fashioned fun."[18] Renewal zones are the "green pastures" and "quiet waters" where God restores survivors' souls. Renewal zones empower us to walk *through* the long-shadowed valley.

Renewal zones may be the beach, a forest, a wood shop, a garden. Or a table shared with a trusted friend at a coffee shop, or quiet moments in a church sanctuary. Some survivors are renewed by a massage, or by participating in a support group, attending a Christmas memorial service, mass on All Souls' Day, or building an altar in the home for the Day of the Dead.

Renewal zones help survivors become more comfortable in the harness of grief and are essential for healthy survival and spirituality.

Busting Taboos

In a sermon in Westminster Abbey that had more impact and drew more interest than he could have imagined, Dean Michael Mayne acknowledged the suicide of his father, a priest, when Michael was three. "It surprised me that so many of those present had relatives, friends, colleagues, who had taken their own life and needed to hear this spoken of openly and within the context of Christian faith."[19] Although Mayne could not remember his father, other than through the photographs he occasionally glanced at, he clearly remembered the consequences of the suicide and the public and ecclesiastical scandal.

Mayne deflated the taboo and allowed his vulnerability to bless others. He commented, "Professionalism so often involves a holding back of large parts of oneself, an avoidance of the vulnerability that can only enhance our ability to be of help if we know, and can show others, how to use it creatively and redemptively."[20]

Sixty years passed. The parish, with a few parishioners who remembered the family, invited Mrs. Mayne, on her 94th birthday, and her children, grandchildren, and great-grandchildren to return for a service of remembrance. They unveiled a stone honoring Reverend Mayne's five years of ministry in that place. Mayne concluded, "Even in the worst of events God is present and there are possibilities of redemption."[21] After a long career of theological reflection, Mayne noted, "I believe that when he [my father] fell to his death he was in the deepest sense caught and held in the everlasting arms of the one who is the merciful and loving Father of us all."[22] Had Mayne not been a suicide survivor could he have reached such a belief in God's generosity?

Mayne's willingness to be vulnerable allowed him to reach out to parishioners whose today resembled his yesterday. Find and make occasions to share your experience as a survivor. What you have learned in this long shadow may be a godsend for someone upon whom the long shadow has recently fallen.

Challenging the Stigma

Survivors must challenge the stigma of suicide. Tom Hennessy, in his newspaper columns, contends that any breakthrough in suicide prevention will come only with the ending of the stigma. Give yourself permission to grieve thoroughly even if it makes others uncomfortable or anxious. Challenge the social silencing of suicide. Challenge the myth of closure. Challenge inadequate government spending for suicide prevention and survivor care. Challenge faith communities to be more compassionate in companioning survivors. Empowerment can be found in John's crisp sentence following the death of Lazarus,

"Jesus wept" (John 11:35). John captured Jesus' response to the grief of Lazarus' sisters, Mary and Martha. "He was deeply moved and troubled" (v. 33). If Jesus can be "deeply moved and troubled" so can his followers!

Reflection: Spend some time meditating on this hymn text by Frances Ridley Havergal:

> Take my life and let it be, consecrated Lord to thee.
> Take my moments and my days,
> Let them flow in ceaseless praise.
> Take my hands, and let them move
> at the impulse of thy love;
> take my heart, it is thine own,
> it shall be thy royal throne.[23]

Think of ways God gives permission to your grief. How might God use your voice, your intellect, your experience in suicide care or in suicide prevention? Reread the text, inserting the word *grief*: "Take my *grief*, and let it be. . . ."

> Prayer: Permission-giver, give me the courage to permission my grief. Bring into my grief those who will support my surviving because they, too, are surviving. Remind me that my feelings as a survivor do not alienate me from you. Amen.

Chapter 4

Reconstructing Meaning After Suicide

There must be some way
to make meaning
out of meaninglessness.
I can live with my grief
if, somehow, I can understand why
she could not live with her life.

> Grieving is the act of affirming or reconstructing a personal world of meaning that has been challenged by loss.
> —Robert Neimeyer[1]

There was nothing to indicate to Joshua Logan, the writer/director of such classic films as *South Pacific, Bus Stop,* and *Mister Roberts,* that this first session with a new psychiatrist would be significant. Having suffered from manic-depressive illness much of his adult life, Logan had seen several therapists. He had just said, "My father died of pneumonia . . . when I was three years old" when the psychiatrist challenged him. "Your father cut his throat with a pocket knife in a sanatorium. I think it's about time you knew that, Mr. Logan." Logan demanded to know the psychiatrist's source of information.

After leaving the appointment, Logan telephoned his uncle Will, who confirmed the accuracy of the psychiatrist's disclosure.

"But they always told me he died of pneumonia," Logan protested. His uncle explained that Logan's father had died of pneumonia— caused by the blood that filled his lungs.

"But why didn't anyone tell me? Why didn't my mother tell me?"

"She never wanted you to know, Josh. I can't tell you why, except I imagine she thought it would be too painful for you."

"It's not painful, Will, it's a relief, because at last I know the truth. The boil has been lanced and the sore is clean. In fact, I'm feeling better than I have in a very long time. Now I know my father, and for the first time in my life. I feel close to him for the first time. He must have been very much like me."

His uncle kindly assured Logan that he and his father were a lot alike. If only the conversation had ended at that point. The uncle closed by cautioning Logan, "And I hope you won't tell your mother you know."[2]

Creating Meaning After Suicide

According to thanatologist Robert Neimeyer, suicide requires survivors to "reconstruct a world that again 'makes sense,' that restores a semblance of meaning, direction and interpretability to a life that is forever transformed."[3] Some individuals cannot make meaning out of a suicide because they are denied component materials—like a note or information from the postmortem—that would facilitate the reconstruction of meaning. Others struggle because they erroneously think they have to find meaning in the suicide and in living after a suicide. Rather, meaning is something survivors *create* with God's generous help.[4]

"I keep going over it in my mind," one survivor told our grief group, "and the suicide just does not make sense. Still does not make any sense." You could understand a surviving parent, spouse, sibling, or friend saying this a day, a week, a month, or even six months after the death. This participant was sharing twenty-five years after her husband's suicide. A son's death in an automobile accident had "rebooted" grief she had long thought settled. Some survivors find that they must reopen the suicide or rewrite the meaning of the suicide at every significant juncture of life's development and transition. Renewing the narrative can happen while making new friends or neighbors, making polite conversation with the new minister, doing a life narrative in a retirement center, or responding to a simple get-to-know-you question, "How many children do you have?" Ever asked that? Sure you have, but you may never have considered how it might resound along the canyons of a survivor's memory. One mother told me,

> Well, it depends on who is asking. If it is "making nice" conversation while waiting for dessert, I'll say two children. But if someone with potential for friendship asks, I tell them, "I have two children living and one in heaven." Then I watch their reaction. If they ask how my son died, I say, "Suicide." Some act as if I had slapped them.

For others, questions about their own understanding of life—of their life up to that moment and their longings for something "more"—prompt them to ask questions long unasked. For Jane Fonda, it was yet another letter from one of her mother's friends—she had thrown away previous letters in which her mother was mentioned. This letter, however, came after Jane had begun writing her autobiography. At age 63 Fonda concluded, "I had reached a point when I knew I would need, at last, to understand my mother."[5] Fonda was stunned.

> Was I crazy never to have seen my mother as three people had now described her: a lively, pleasure-loving, iconic rock of a woman? Why had I remembered her only as a sad, nervous victim to whom I would no more turn for help than try to walk on quicksand, whom I desperately did not want to be like?[6]

A year after conversations with her mother's friends prodded an altered perspective, Jane read her mother's medical files. In an eight-page essay that Frances had typed after being admitted to the mental hospital, Jane discovered that her grandfather had spanked the children "often and hard," in a manner that would today qualify as abuse.

As her grandfather lost his sanity, only the piano tuner was allowed to come to the house. Her father's trusted friend sexually molested 8-year-old Frances. At age 65, Fonda concluded, "This trauma colored her life, and mine."[7]

Slowly, the "pieces fell into place" for this daughter who had been 12 years old when her mother suicided. Fonda dedicated her memoirs, "And here's to you, Frances Ford Seymour—my mother—you did the best you could. You gave me life; you gave me wounds; you also gave me a part of what I needed to grow stronger at the broken places."[8]

Jane did not discover meaning until she began weaving the loss into her own life story. Said differently, writing about these discoveries caused her to reinterpret the meaning she had initially assigned to her mother's suicide.

Three Levels of Meaning

Survivors face three levels of meaning: temporary, transitional, and transformational. Temporary meanings are those initial meanings "assigned" to a suicide—sometimes seized like a life raft because we are fatigued or numb. They are often helpful at first, but they commonly need to change over time.

Transitional meanings are those meanings we live our way into as the smoke clears on this event that has made chaos in our lives. Some survivors initially conclude, "He did it to hurt *me!*" That contention, rehearsed to anyone who will listen, gets survivors through the funeral and the first months. Then someone challenges that interpretation and, perhaps, nudges us toward another. Robert Neimeyer, a survivor, contends, "Early provisional meanings of the death tend to be revisited as the reality of living with loss raises new questions and undermines old answers."[9] Josh Logan's long-held "provisional meanings" of his father's death were overturned by one psychiatrist's candor.

Transformational meanings are those we craft on the forge of life. Leonard Maholick, a psychiatrist and friend, walked into the Bolton home soon after Mitch Bolton ended his life in February 1977. He urged the family to honor their grief and to make decisions together, then suggested, "There is a gift in your son's death. You may not believe it at this bitter moment, but it is authentic and it can be yours if you are willing to search for it."[10] Mitch Bolton's mother, Iris, described her initial response to Maholick's assertion:

> I gasped! He was saying that my pain was a gift, that the dislocation of so many lives caused by my son's careless and selfish termination of all earthly responsibilities, was a gift. I saw in memory the naked body on the hospital table. . . . Was this doctor saying that was a gift?

Dr. Maholick explained,

> This gift will not jump out at you or thrust itself into your life. You must search for it. As time passes, you will be amazed at unanticipated opportunities for helping yourself and others that will come your way, because of Mitch. Today, you probably need to condemn him. It's only natural. But I earnestly believe that one day you will be able to acknowledge his gift.[11]

Three years passed. Early one morning, Dr. Maholick called Iris Bolton to ask if she would talk to a mother whose daughter had just suicided. Iris and the other mother spoke for hours on the phone, and then Iris spent time with the family. If Iris Bolton had accepted as final her temporary or transitional meanings of her son's death, she would have been unable to make a difference to this family. She talked to them about "the gift," just as her psychiatrist had talked to her. The girl's stepfather snapped, "You mean Julie's killing herself is some kind of crazy gift to Cathy or me? I don't believe it." Bolton delicately responded, "Bill, it's not that her death is like a going-away present, all boxed and gift-wrapped. Her gift is within you and you will find it only when you decide what to do with this experience."[12]

Iris knew how outrageous the idea sounded, so she explained that the concept was like a protective umbrella in her "knotted agony." Then she acknowledged:

It was hard for me, too. I share it with you as a hope to hang onto. I'm here right now only because of my son's suicide. His act directed me into a line of work I'd never even dreamed of before. I had to work to discover his gift, but here I am with the privilege of knowing you and being with you in your grief. That's a real gift to me and in turn, it helps me with my own healing process. And I am thankful for it.[13]

Thirty years have passed since Mitch's death. Iris Bolton has talked to and listened to hundreds of families and thousands more through her book *My Son . . . My Son*. Bolton, over time, lived her way into a transformational meaning because she did not settle for the temporary or transitional meanings.

Readiness for Meaning

Meaning did not come for Jane Fonda until she gained access to her mother's medical records. Such data often provide pieces that, like the scraps that form a quilt, must be fitted together to create a single, comprehensible piece.

I closed Mother's medical records and lay in bed feeling indescribably sad for her and at the same time utterly relieved. I wished I could fold her in my arms, rock her, and tell her how everything was all right, that I loved her and forgave her because now I understood. Finally. I understood the nature of one of the shadows that I inherited from her that has incubated in my body for so long.[14]

That realization led Fonda, who for ten years had been studying child abuse, to perceive her mother differently and to interpret the suicide differently. Frances, she lovingly concluded, had been "a victim, a beautiful but damaged butterfly, unable to give me what I needed—to be loved, seen—because she could not give it to herself."[15] An Asian proverb seems timely: "When the student is ready, the teacher will come."

When the survivor is ready to face hard, discomforting questions, meaning will show up. Meaning often comes out of what Frederick Buechner calls "rich human compost."[16] Meaning also comes after we ask God to empower us to face the hard, unanswerable questions, and to keep asking them.

One night a participant in my grief group turned to another and asked, "You said that both of your parents died in May. Was it an automobile accident?"

"No, my father shot my mother and then turned the gun on himself." That sparse response, offered without hesitation, sucked all the energy out of the room. Inwardly, I wanted to applaud. This disclosure marked an achievement, for Bev had never disclosed anything more than "my parents died in May." She had not, until this moment, summoned the courage to voice words to wrap around the loss. These words, her husband told me, represented a significant embrace of the reality from which she was seeking to create meaning.

Some survivors function like an amateur Detective Lieutenant Columbo, sifting through papers in desks and safety deposit boxes, questioning friends and work colleagues, sifting again and again through the details, "one more time," seeking without success to uncover the "clue" that has, thus far, eluded them. The lack of an "Aha!" moment prevents meaning from being formed or reformed.

Meaning-making is a hard, demanding task. Some survivors say it is necessarily done as if in slow motion, editing frame by frame, like watching a surveillance tape and stopping to zoom in on key details. Some survivors become like grand juries weighing evidence to support an indictment, if not a conviction of someone who caused the suicide, or someone who contributed to it, or failed to prevent the suicide, or failed to acknowledge the severity of the individual's suicidal intentions.

Some of the search for a meaning can become complicated in the absence of clear evidence of the intention to suicide. Survivors sometimes ignore or recast the evidence of intention: "He was cleaning the gun and it discharged." When the investigation is inconclusive, survivors live with ambiguity and a menacing question: Was it *really* suicide?

I once attended a memorial service that was clouded with loss. Kevin was HIV-positive and had long medical charts filled with the host of illnesses he had battled. One friend contended that Kevin had always bounced back, and he had seemed to be "his old self" that last night. He kept insisting on visiting "one more bar." Kevin was drunk, but insisted that he could drive home. One friend followed him for a couple of blocks before reminding himself that "Kevin could drive better after drinking than some could who had not touched a drop." Kevin pulled into his garage and closed the door.

Everyone agreed on those facts. But "the facts" led friends to different conclusions. One said, "I think he wanted to die. I think Kevin wanted one last night on the town with friends for old times' sake. I think he knew exactly what he was doing. He had seen a dozen friends die awful deaths. But he did not want to leave proof—like a hose connected to the exhaust." Another was adamant: "Suicide. No way! Kevin was feeling much better. He had talked to his accountant and lawyer that week about re-opening his business. He had everything to live for."

Kevin's friends scripted and rescripted the "facts." In some ways, it was like redealing cards in a tense game of poker. The leading contention—some would say the necessary one in a "friends don't let friends drive drunk" world—was that he expended so much mental energy driving home that he passed out once he concluded he was safely in his garage. Unfortunately, he had not turned off the motor.

Close friends were anxious to be exonerated of any complicity in Kevin's death. It was only sometime later that one friend spun this dissenting meaning. "He took his life. AIDS would have eventually taken him and he had walked so many friends through their final illnesses and it had not been pretty. He wanted death on his terms. All that talk about 'reopening his business' was just guys making each other feel better."

Another insisted, "We are *not* responsible. Even if I had driven him home and gotten him to bed—which I had done on other occasions— he would have found another way. He chose to beat the virus to the last punch."

Meaning will not always stay meaningful. Meaning has a way of unraveling, then rebuilding in a new form.

The Extravagant Mercy of God

I attended a young man's funeral. Speculation swirled about the motivation for his death, but friends assured me that there would be no mention of the word suicide in this carefully scripted service. The minister, however, surprised everyone. "Ever since I was notified of Ryan's death, I have struggled to make sense of it. 'Why, Ryan, why!?' I have asked that question over and over."

The minister helped a struggling congregation come to the edge of meaning by saying, "Today I want each of us to make one commitment to Ryan that we will do whatever we have to do—when we know, or believe, someone is depressed—to get them help. We will do whatever we have to do, even if it risks the relationship, so that there will not be another Ryan and a church filled on a Tuesday afternoon with friends asking, 'Why? *Why?*'"

If those in attendance keep that promise, Ryan's death will feed a stream of meaning.

After reading Jane Fonda's words on her prolonged pursuit of meaning-making, I remembered Albert Hsu's insight, "If we go on living, we will do so as people who see the world very differently."[17] Notice those first five words: *if* we go on living. We must choose to move forward, to grow, from this point, from this death.

Robert Neimeyer compares survivors' lives to a novel that loses a central character. The life disrupted by suicide "forces its 'author' to envision potentially far-reaching changes in plot in order for the story to move forward."[18] Continual revisions may be required to achieve a satisfying level of meaning. Over time, Neimeyer suggests, survivors need to jettison, revise, or deepen their concept of meaning.

I find support for this in the Book of James: "If any of you lacks wisdom, he should ask God, who gives generously to all without finding fault" (James 1:5, NIV). Substitute *meaning* for *wisdom* and reread the sentence. God will companion survivors on the path to meaning.

This was modeled in Jesus' post-Resurrection encounter with two grieving disciples on the Emmaus Road. Jesus could have said, "Boo, it's me! I have been raised from the dead!" Rather he chose to walk "along with them" (about seven miles), nudging them to share what was on their minds: "What are you discussing together as you walk along?" (Luke 24:17).

Survivors cannot easily make meaning out of death by suicide without God's help—which may come through psychological support, reflection, and time. Rabbi Samuel Karff observes, "Many find it difficult to embrace the fundamental premise of classic Western religion: that there is a God who created us; that there is a God who cares for us; and that there is a God who guides and helps us on our earthly journey."[19] It is often hard for postmodern survivors to believe that God wants to partner with them in the making of meaning. Yet God guides us on the journey to meaning, even when it has detours. God walks with us in our troubles to bring us to greater freedom. God, Rabbi Karff contends, "frees me from the Egypts of my life."[20]

I do not believe it is coincidental that as Jane Fonda decided to reexamine her mother's death, her mother's friend was writing her one more time. God was stirring the unrest in Jane Fonda's heart and the longing in the friend's heart.

What might God do in your life? Who might God bring into your life with raw resources for the making of meaning? Who might walk "along with you" on your Emmaus Road? How comfortable would you feel asking for help?

In a real way, we keep our dead alive by asking questions, by reassembling wonderings the way a quilter tries out fabrics. Frederick Buechner's father suicided when he was a boy—actually, on the day he had promised to take Frederick and his brother to a football game.

> We didn't talk about my father with each other, and we didn't talk about him outside the family either partly at least because suicide was looked on as something a little shabby and shameful in those days. . . . His suicide was a secret we nonetheless

tried to keep as best we could, and after a while my father himself became such a secret. There were times when he almost seemed a secret we were trying to keep from each other. . . . And because words are so much a part of what we keep the past alive by, if only words to ourselves, by not speaking of what we remembered about him we soon simply stopped remembering at all, or at least I did.[21]

Sometimes survivors first live with the misery, then with mystery, and, in time—a dimension of time that can be excruciatingly slow—live their ways into meaning. Sixty-three years later, Buechner concluded, "I suppose one way to read my whole life—my religious faith, the books I have written, the friends I have made—is as a search for him."[22]

William Cowper penned lyrics that have encouraged many survivors.

God moves in a mysterious way
his wonders to perform
he plants his footsteps in the sea,
and rides upon the storm.

Blind unbelief is sure to err,
and scan his work in vain;
God is his own interpreter,
and he will make it plain.[23]

Meaning is created, ultimately, in the outrageously extravagant mercy of God. Mercy, even on good days, may stump us. Take a moment and reflect on your willingness to wait knowing "he will make it plain."

Reflection: Job 42 includes the poignant observation, "The Lord blessed the latter part of Job's life more than the first" (42:12). In what ways can you imagine the Lord blessing you as you create meaning in your equivalent of "the latter part"?

Prayer: Meaning-giver, you know my longing for this to be "made plain." You long to be involved in our struggle to creating meaning out of inherited chaos. You never scold us for our persistence in seeking meaning. Nudge us closer to meaning, even when it seems concealed and hidden. Amen.

Chapter 5

Surviving Suicide's Assault on Our Assumptions and Values

I am grieving
a long list of never-to-be's,
events forever denied me by this suicide:
baptisms, graduations,
marriages, grandchildren,
postcards from far-flung places;
awards, honors, and achievements
that would have made us proud.
Christmas celebrations around fireplaces,
candles blown out on birthday cakes,
photographs on desks and den tables.
All my cherished assumptions
about how life would unfold
went with him to the grave.
I am already anticipating his absence
in the sunset of my life.

> [Suicide] can validate/invalidate the constructions on the
> basis of which we live, or it may stand as a novel experience
> for which we have no constructions.
> —*Robert Neimeyer*[1]

Helen was a newlywed when the stock market crashed in 1929. Like
many couples, she and her husband assumed they could "live on love."
Many women lost husbands, and children lost fathers, in those dark

months of financial chaos. Fortunes and economic security vanished in a matter of hours. Assumptions about life and the future were swallowed by market forces. The economic chaos and the prevailing cultural mandate that "he's not much of a man who cannot provide for his family" drove Helen's husband to end his life in 1932. This young bride went to work and became a successful lampshade designer, advertising manager, and bookkeeper. In her new life in the long shadow of grief, she made time after work to write inspirational poetry. If someone had asked Helen Steiner Rice, as she stood at her husband's grave, if she would survive this, how could she have answered in her numbness? Could she have believed that good things that would come to her in a radically altered future? Could she have believed that her words would become deep wells of inspiration for millions of future survivors and grievers?[2]

Humans and Our Assumptions

Humans live according to cherished assumptions that give life meaning and direction. According to Robert Neimeyer:

> In the course of daily living, each of us ordinarily is sustained
> by the network of habitual explanations, expectations, and
> enactments that shape our lives with others. These tacit as-
> sumptions provide us with a basic sense of order regarding
> our pasts, familiarity regarding our current relationships, and
> predictability regarding our futures.[3]

British psychiatrist Colin Murray Parks identifies assumptions as our "internal models" or frameworks in which we sort and match "incoming data in order to orient the self, recognize what is happening, and plan" appropriate responses to life's realities.[4] Before we respond to certain stimuli or experiences, our assumptions initially shape and guide us. Humans are deeply attached to their assumptions and to their right to make and maintain assumptions. Individuals assume that others will honor their assumptions.

Events such as suicide "can challenge the adequacy of our most cherished beliefs and taken-for-granted ways of living."[5] Assumptions provide structure and act as a mental and spiritual shorthand. Assumptions provide stability and a measure of predictability. Suicide can impact our assumptions the way a well-struck cue ball sends billiard balls careening on a pool table. Any death that is at odds with our core values, beliefs, and self-identifications, a death that does not make sense, particularly a suicide, topples our assumptions like a house of cards.

"I assumed . . ."

I assumed that because I had signed a contract with Cowley this book would be published.

I assumed because I had written other books, I would complete this manuscript.

I assumed the draft I submitted would be evaluated as "insightful, well-written, psychologically and theologically sound."

I assumed I would live long enough to see this manuscript to publication.

One must be careful about investing too zealously in assumptions. Like spirited adolescents in love, they will break your heart. Sooner or later humans discover that assumptions are composed of the most fragile of fabrics.

"I just assumed we would grow old together."

"I assumed the psychiatrist knew what she was doing."

"I assumed he was taking his meds."

"I assumed she was just being dramatic."

Sooner or later humans take the broom and dustpan to the shattered shards of cherished assumptions.

Take a moment and think about the assumptions that were operative in your life before the suicide. How have your assumptions changed? Just as we must pack a loved one's possessions into boxes to be given away, sold, or stored, we must attend to once-valued, now-deflated assumptions that litter our emotional and spiritual landscapes.

"I *assumed* suicide could not happen in our family."

"I *assumed* she would never . . ."

"I *assumed* we would dance together at our son's wedding."

"I *assumed* God would never let this happen to us."

"I *assumed* . . ."

I *assumed* I had a right to make assumptions.

Suicide can turn our assumptions and values inside out and leave hearts spinning. As assumptions collapse, like a chain of dominos, confident individuals are dumbfounded. Individuals who have functioned as the rock in a family, a network of friends, a religious community, or an institution are made helpless.

Assumptions can be deflated like balloons or tires. Suicide especially can squash almost any assumption, at least temporarily. Maybe you assumed that God would "save" your loved one. Maybe you assumed a friend would "be there" for you. Maybe you assumed your partner would honor differences in your grief styles. Maybe you assumed that certain individuals would never be uncomfortable with you mentioning your loved one's name or recognizing a significant anniversary in your grief narrative. Maybe you assumed that family, friends, colleagues, fellow pew-sharers would honor your longing for remembering this loved one.

Maybe you assumed that "time heals." Maybe you assumed that if you were a nice, compliant survivor who read the books and articles, showed up for appointments with counselors, and participated in grief groups, you would someday be "done" with grief and would heal from this wounding of the spirit. You would join the legions of ex-grievers. You assumed that you, your spouse, your family would "get back to normal."

Shattered assumptions are the "morning breath" of the emotions. Many survivors are made to feel incompetent—even foolish—for having invested in them.

Life in a Strange Land

Centuries ago, a psalmist voiced the question asked by so many exiled Jews, "How do we sing the Lord's song in a strange land?" (137:4). Suicide launches an emotional and spiritual exile from everything familiar, from deeply held assumptions. Recall that Albert Hsu, after his father's suicide, observed, "If we go on living, we will do so as people who see the world very differently."[6] Along with many other changes, some survivors' assumptions about God alter dramatically. One griever said, "God has never been the same. Where was the 'all-powerful God' when my son pulled the trigger? God couldn't have prevented this?"

Another assumption, one that is sometimes prized even if it is unstated or understated, is that "we are/were a *normal* family." Suicide puts the family immediately under the speculative gaze of friends, neighbors, and community. "Whether intentional or not," Baugher and Jordan note, "some people ask questions and say things that suggest blame, neglect, or some failure on your part."[7] Some individuals feel the need to offer commentary on a suicide, particularly a public suicide. Vince Foster's death fueled endless insensitive speculations by political pundits. His widow, Lisa, who must have assumed that her privacy would be honored, had to endure repeated investigations, exposés, and books by scandalmongers.

Survivors survive the collapse of their assumptions in small increments of time: hours, half-days, days. They may feel pressured to deny or disguise their grief because some friends are so devoted to the "moving on" mentality.

Survivors may not be expected by others to "sing the Lord's song." But other people *will* assume that survivors should in due course demonstrate that they are over the death. But with our assumptions shattered by death, we remain in the strange land of life after suicide long after most believe we have returned from exile.

The Assumption That Grief Is to Be "Gotten Over"

Survivors, too, sometimes assume that grief is a race to "Over-It-Land." Those with a competitive streak may have a need to see who can be the first to reach this assumed goal. One might almost hear the cheerleaders shouting, "You can do it!" "Come on, come on. Shake a leg!"

Unlike a footrace, the finish line for survivors keeps being moved.

And there are days—even moments—in which any finish line seems to be a shimmering mirage on the horizon. The griever thinks she is doing well, but then, for any number of reasons, a setback occurs.

Spiritually and emotionally wise survivors do not "get over" a suicide. Survivors do not get back to normal. Survivors do not "move on" as rapidly and efficiently as some expect. Survivors do, with God's help, move forward. Judy Collins, after the death of her son Clark, noted:

> In the aftermath of his suicide, all perceptions changed, all bets were off as to how we, together and individually, could weather the storm of being suicide survivors. We knew nothing about how to do it. We only knew we had lost our most beloved son, father, husband, cousin, nephew, friend. Ten years later, we are learning how in the world to do this, to be suicide survivors.[8]

Some would grouse at Judy Collins's admission and indict her for incompetent grieving. "What! Ten years and she's not over it! She just has not tried hard enough. She just does not *want* to be over it!"

The great unspoken assumption is that *any* grief is to be "gotten over." Peggy Anderson, after her husband's suicide, wrote, "I have come to realize that you don't get over your grief; you just get to a different phase."[9] Kay Redfield Jamison, a psychiatrist and survivor, insists, "No one has ever found a way to heal the hearts or settle the minds of those left behind in its dreadful wake."[10] Some who have experienced other losses have assumed that suicide grief is like any other grief—an assumption that falls apart in the face of experience. Many survivors report that suicide grief is like no other grief.

Survival becomes a basic stream in a life story, sometimes resumed after significant pauses, interruptions, detours. One father reflected, in the ashes of his assumptions,

> Everything, at least every important thing that happens to us, is a snippet in our continued story, the life story we are writing

with our choices. Every episode in our story becomes the raw material for the next episode. And what we write next depends on how we interpret the previous chapter.[11]

The future is determined by how we interpret the collapse of assumptions. The future does not depend on an individual's actions or decisions but rather on our responses in the absence of familiar assumptions.

"I Have Survived"

Some survivors need a moment deep in a wood, high in the sand overlooking a beach, in a mountain meadow—or in the stress of a sleepless midnight—when they inform themselves: I will, by God's grace, survive this. Others conclude angrily, "By god, I will survive this!" That's what Alice Roosevelt Longworth, Theodore Roosevelt's daughter, concluded after her son-in-law died and immediately after Paulina, her daughter, suicided by washing down sixty barbiturates with liquor in 1957. Alice totally reorganized her life to care for Joanna, her 10-year-old granddaughter. She undertook a new chapter in her life. All her assumptions about her "old age" vanished![12]

A quote I often share with grievers is from the experience of Eleanor Roosevelt, well acquainted with grief and survival. Her parents and a brother died by her tenth birthday. The first Franklin D. Roosevelt, Jr., died as an infant. In 1945, when she became a presidential widow, she rebuffed a reporter's curiosity about her future with a terse reply: "The story is over." Most Americans expected her, like other widowed former First Ladies, to withdraw from the public eye. Instead, at President Truman's insistence, she served as an Ambassador to the United Nations and drafted the Universal Declaration of Human Rights. She later reflected on her experience:

> You gain strength, courage, and confidence by every experience in which you really stop to look fear in the face. You are

able to say to yourself, "I will live through this horror. I can take the next thing that comes along . . ." You must do the thing you think you cannot do.[13]

Many individuals have survived to conclude, "I have survived *this*. I have done the thing I did not think I could do."

Reflection: Take some moments to ponder Eleanor Roosevelt's words, "You must do the thing you think you cannot do." What have you told yourself you cannot do?

> Prayer: One Beyond All Assumptions, in the tumult of suicide, you call me, in experiences I cannot understand—experiences I doubt that I can survive, to trust you. By [name's] action, I am forced to reexamine what I believed and what I now believe, what I assumed and what I now assume. Help me examine fragile assumptions; reacquaint me with how unbreakable is your love. Show me hints of a future. Give us the courage to mourn my loved one *and* my assumptions. Amen.

Chapter 6

Rehabilitating Judas

Forgive seems to be a word
stuck in my heart.
There had been so many
"kiss, make up, forgive" moments in our relationship. Too many.
I feel betrayed.
This one will take a long time because if
it takes two to forgive, I'll have to forgive for both of us.

> [O]ur mother approached our father's lifeless body,
> touched him, and then recoiled in horror and a convul-
> sion of tears. With that one abrupt gesture, most of what
> constituted the themes of our family narrative were swept
> away, and we were thrown collectively into a tumultuous
> renegotiation of who we were, how we would manage, and
> what his death meant.
> —*Robert Neimeyer*[1]

Judas kept wandering through Jackie Kennedy's mind in those first
pain-drenched days of initial widowhood following the President's as-
sassination in November 1963. Actually, she juggled dual griefs: her
newborn son, Patrick Bouvier Kennedy—only two days old—had died
in August 1963. At Bobby Kennedy's request, Father Richard McSorley,
a priest at Georgetown University, briefly counseled the former First
Lady in 1964. Long after her death, and a year after McSorley's death,
his papers, archived at Georgetown University, disclosed the depth
of Jackie's anguish. Jackie had asked him, "I feel as though I am going

out of my mind at times. Wouldn't God understand that I just want to be with him [Jack]?" Then she added, "Do you think that God would separate me from my husband if I killed myself?" McSorley gently reminded her that their children, Caroline and John, needed her. He reminded her of the great Christian hope in resurrection.[2]

Jackie's intense fear of hell, of experiencing what she believed to be Judas' fate, drowned out the siren call of suicide. Maybe our assumptions about Judas' eternal destiny—and they are only assumptions because the Bible does not say Judas went to hell—have prevented a lot of suicides. Seen in this light, our traditional understanding of Judas may have helped save lives.

However, Judas' portrayal as a traitor condemned by God has also perpetuated hurtful stereotypes and assumptions about others who suicide. Judas has been maligned by centuries of agenda-laden interpretation, much of which may be historically erroneous. David Reed charges that too many ideas about Judas are based on contemporary North Atlantic concepts of suicide rather than those of the first-century Mediterranean world.[3] Caroline Whelan, after examining 900 suicides in antiquity, noted that suicide would not have been "understood" in that time as a negative choice.[4]

What if Judas has been enjoying afternoon tea with new arrivals in heaven for two millennia?

Another Side to the Story

Harley Harrison III was the lawyer every defendant wanted; even if your mother acknowledged your guilt, Harlan would defend you. In one celebrated episode, after the state had presented a strong case, Harley approached the jury to open his defense. "Ladies and gentlemen, from all I've heard in this courtroom, my client is guilty. As guilty as hell." He paused as his client gasped. "If you believe the evidence the prosecutor has presented. Yes sir, 'as guilty as hell!,' but *only if* you believe the state's case. I ask you to *consider* the possibility there's another side of the story. My client's side." Perhaps Judas deserves such a defense as well. We may have only heard one side of his case.

If Judas had not existed, the church would have invented him. Quite frankly, the church needed a scapegoat to distract from the miserable betrayals by the other disciples. I grew up as a fundamentalist Christian, and in that context there was never any doubt that Judas was "as guilty as hell," as one uncle muttered under his breath following a sermon on Judas' "pathetic" life. Under our steeple no one would tolerate anything that sounded like mercy toward the "bastard disciple." The Betrayer. Every Lent, Judas became the whipping boy and stimulated a fervent recitation of the numerous ways "we, too, betray Jesus." Actually, for me, Judas has been a puzzlement. If we are redeemed by Jesus' death, how could the fact that Judas handed him over make him such a vile, heinous villain?

I never heard anything that even sounded like a kind word toward Judas until, as an adult, I heard a guest minister offer a fresh look at the betrayer. I cannot remember his three points, or his illustrations, but I remember thinking that he was one courageous preacher. He was, unfortunately, never invited to preach again in our church. Do not mess with people's heads about Judas!

Every Lent, my mind drifts to Judas, the misunderstood, misguided disciple. I have spent long hours reading theological works in search of clues to understand him. I have spent hours reflecting on Judas. That reading and reflecting fed a discontent in me as I wrote this book. I cannot understand why Judas has been portrayed as "the bad boy" disciple.

In Acts 1, ten days after Jesus' ascension to heaven, Peter castigates Judas. But Peter is hardly in a position to lambaste Judas for betrayal. Judas at least had acknowledged to Jesus' enemies, "I know him." Peter, on the other hand, had vigorously insisted, "I *do not* know him." Rereading Acts, I become suspicious of Peter's intent. I sense a "spin" unfolding. While I concede that Jesus had appointed Peter to be "the rock," or leader of the disciples, I wish, in the magnificent glow of Jesus' post-resurrection grace, that Peter, as recipient of such responsibility, would have been more tolerant of his co-betrayer. Although he did not use the word *betrayed*, Peter deflected any criticism of himself by indicting Judas as the one "who served as guide for those who arrested Jesus" (Acts 1:16). But the Roman authorities and Jewish leaders did not need a guide to find Jesus. Where Jesus prayed was not exactly a secret.

Many of Jesus' followers—perhaps most—deserted Jesus in his moments of ultimate agony. One even streaked away nude. There were no heroes that dark night.

Truth be told, after any suicide, finger-pointing is a dangerous and unproductive business. It is unfortunate that Peter fell into the trap of looking for someone to blame.

Was It Betrayal? (And Other Thoughts That Challenge Assumptions)

For centuries, the church has used Judas to justify its outrageous lack of grace toward suicide. I would like to talk to Judas. I would like to hear his side of the story. It would not surprise me in the least to find Judas on heaven's official welcoming committee. Imagine clergy who have worked themselves up annually eviscerating the twelfth disciple, encountering him in their first moments in eternity's dawn. "Judas is my name. What's yours?"

At the funeral of General William Westmoreland, who led U.S. troops in Vietnam, Bishop C. Fitzsimmons Allison sought to stretch the congregation's evaluation of the life of the General. Vietnam, he noted, was just one chapter in Westmoreland's long military career. Allison closed his funeral homily by asserting that God, not the critics, the media, or historians, will have the "last word" on the value of an individual's life.[5]

Those are fine, grace-laced words that suicide survivors can appropriate.

I concede that I have no credentials as a New Testament scholar (although, to be sure, the scholars in the last twenty-five years have not expended much energy reexamining Judas). But for me, Paul wrote words that are like a magnet drawing survivors to grace. In prefacing his remarks on the Eucharist, Paul wrote, "For I received from the Lord what I passed on to you. The Lord Jesus Christ, on the night he was *betrayed*, took bread . . ." (1 Corinthians 11:23). Note that Paul does not indict Judas: "On the night the Lord Jesus Christ was betrayed *by that dastardly Judas. . . .*" Paul goes on to quote Jesus as saying, "Do this . . . in remembrance of me" (v. 25). If we "remember" not just Jesus' death, but his life, and resurrection as well, we can discern in these words the generous, outrageously extravagant forgiveness that he modeled.

In addition, as some scholars have argued, the English word *betrayed* has contemporary linguistic and theological implications that may not apply to what Paul wrote. Bishop John Shelby Spong argues that *paradidonai*, the Greek word used by Paul, more accurately means "handed over," which has different implications than the more preju-dicial *betrayed*. Paul wrote, "Jesus was *delivered over* [*paradidonai*] to death for our sins and raised to life for our justification" (Romans 4:25). Four chapters later, Paul declared, "He who did not spare his own Son, but *gave him up* [*paradidonai*] for us all—how will he not also, along with him, graciously give us all things?" (8:32). Noted scholar William Klassen insists, "This widespread variation in usage of the term suggests caution in translating *paradidonai* as 'betray.'" Klassen concludes, "The tradition of Judas as betrayer was not found in Paul or in the earliest layers of the tradition."[6]

Readers may need to be reminded that Paul wrote 1 Corinthians about twenty years before the Gospel of Mark, the earliest gospel, was written down. We may speculate that the earliest believers and con-verts "heard" the Easter narrative without any prejudicial denuncia-tion of Judas. Spong asserts:

> It is worth noting in his entire written corpus Paul gives no evidence that he was aware of a betrayal that took place at the hand of one of the twelve disciples, but the English translators knew the later gospel stories, and so they placed that meaning into their rendition of the word. It is one of many examples in which later Christians were guilty of reading Paul through the eyes of the Gospel narrative.[7]

Spong cites another troublesome passage Paul had "received": "That Christ died for our sins according to the Scriptures, that he was buried, that he was raised on the third day . . . and that he appeared to Peter," who had vigorously denied him, *and then to the Twelve*" (1 Corinthians 15:3-5). *Twelve?* Is this a mistake? We have been led to believe that there were only eleven post-Resurrection disciples. Did Paul mean to say *the Eleven?* Chronologically it would be weeks before Matthias joined the newly constituted Twelve. If Judas were dead, why the mention of "the Twelve" here? Although Matthew says, "Then the *eleven* disciples went to Galilee, to the mountain where Jesus had told them to go" (Matthew 28:16), that was written four decades after Paul wrote his narrative.

The significant discrepancy between the description in Matthew's Gospel and the description in Acts 1 also troubles me: "He went away and hanged himself" (Matthew 27:5) and "He fell headlong, his body burst open and all his intestines spilled out" (Acts 1:18). How can two divergent reports be reconciled for a generation that watches TV crime scene investigators "resolve" such differences? I have been amused by the creativity of commentators attempting to reconcile the accounts while retaining their disgust for Judas, some-times using Webster's definitions to qualify his "betrayal" as "lacking genuineness." One preacher, desperately trying to explain, opined, "Apparently the rope broke. When Judas' body hit the ground, his guts burst open." Perhaps, if Judas had hung himself one hundred feet above the ground . . .

Moreover, how do we reconcile Peter's assertion, "With the reward he got for his wickedness [i.e., in handing over Jesus], Judas bought a field" (Acts 1:18) with "He went away and hanged himself" (Matthew 27:5)? How does a dead man buy a field? And as Barbara Essex com-mented in *Bad Boys of the Bible*, "Thirty pieces of silver were barely a day's wages."[8] How much field could that buy?

The more I reflect on Judas—and the more I discover about human nature—the more this discredited "bad boy" disciple gains my sympa-thy. Is Judas the scapegoat designated to divert attention from Peter? Did early Christians collude to divert attention from the misdeeds of their leaders before the resurrection?

A close reading of the biblical texts has called into question whether Judas literally "betrayed" Jesus. It has called into question the nature of his death. A close reading will also reveal that it is questionable to assume that Judas, or anyone else who commits suicide, is condemned to hell.

The Gospel of Matthew reports, simply: "He went away and hanged himself" (27:5). There is not even the hint of eternal condemnation in the passage. This is consistent with other biblical suicides. Scholar David Reed notes that in the narratives of the six suicides reported in the Hebrew Bible, the reader encounters no condemnation of the individual, just a reporting of the cause of death.[9] Unfortunately, this has not kept Christians from hammering family members who are suicide survivors with the certain judgment, "Your loved one went to hell."

What are we to make of Matthew's description of the last hours of Judas?

> When Judas, who had betrayed him, saw that Jesus was condemned, he was seized with remorse and returned the thirty silver coins to the chief priests and the elders. "I have sinned," he said, "for I have betrayed innocent blood." (27:3–4)

That's your responsibility and problem, the Jewish authorities retorted. "So," Matthew reports, "Judas threw the money into the temple and left" (v. 5). How much more flesh from Judas' hide and how much more verbalized remorse do we want from Judas to ignore this repentance, this conversion? Not many people these days are *seized* by remorse. We forget that the father, in the story of the prodigal son, interrupted his son's well-rehearsed confession and simply bestowed grace. Some people then, and some today, prefer to demand a pound of flesh instead. Did Jesus, when he told the story of the prodigal son, want Judas and the other disciples to hear the promise of forgiveness the parable exudes?

God's Extravagant Grace

It can be argued that centuries of misreading Paul and other scriptures in regard to Judas, the betrayal of Jesus, the death of Judas, and suicide in general, have led Christians to wound survivors of suicide and to rein in the very grace offered by the God they proclaim. But God's grace is so outrageously extravagant that heaven will not be heaven if *all* of God's redeemed are not present. That is perhaps the reason I wept at mass the first time I heard the hymn, "O God, You Search Me." Bernadette Farrell wrote, paraphrasing Psalm 139,

There is nowhere on earth I can escape you,
Even the darkness is radiant in your sight.

If darkness is radiant, that includes the survivor's darkness. At that mass, because of the long lines of people approaching the Eucharistic table, we sang the verses again: "God of my present, my past and future, too."[10] These words urge us to see the breadth of God's enduring love for us all, however we die.

People who make the ultimate final choice and take their own lives may well have been taught that by doing so they would die alienated from God. But maybe, just maybe, they discover God's welcoming presence in those first miniseconds of eternity. An unknown Franciscan monk first told a story of a man who, after suicide, found himself in God's presence. The man, overwhelmed by fear of God's wrath, heard God say, "It was tough down there, wasn't it? I know. My son had a tough time of it. Welcome home." Why may this not be how we imagine life after death?

One can almost hear God saying, "Shhh" as the suicide tries to explain why she took her life. We are home. We have arrived in the kingdom of peace. The psalmist's words become reality: "Your hand will lead me, and your right hand will hold me fast" (139:10).

A spirituality of God's extravagant grace makes room for the redemption of Judas that somehow did not make the canon of scripture or the tradition of the church. I believe that the final word has not been written on Judas or on the "wideness" of Jesus' grace. John noted, "Jesus did many other things as well. If every one of them were written down, I suppose that even the whole world would not have room for the books that would be written" (21:25).

Nor has the final word been written on anyone who has suicided. Frederick William Faber, writing from within the mid-nineteenth century's narrow understanding of grace, might have been ahead of his day when he penned:

> There's a wideness in God's mercy like the wideness of the sea;
> there's a kindness in his justice, which is more than liberty.

> There is welcome for the sinner, and more graces for the good;
> there is mercy with the Savior; there is healing in his [love].

> For the love of God is broader than the measure of the mind;
> and the heart of the Eternal is more wonderfully kind.[11]

Jesus once warned that it would be rough being a disciple. He frequently explained to his followers that the way in which he led them was full of difficulty (Matthew 8:20; Matthew 16:24; Mark 14:27). "This very night you will all fall away on account of me," he said to them as his own death neared (Matthew 26:31). Yet we know that, even when abandoned by his disciples, Jesus received them again. Peter knowingly denied Jesus three times and was forgiven—he was even given the chance to lead the church (Luke 22:34–62; John 21:15–19). But no grace for Judas? I do not think so.

I am moved by Matthew Bridges's words in the Easter hymn "Crown Him with Many Crowns":

> who every grief hath known
> that wrings the human breast,
> and takes and bears them for his own,
> that all in him may rest."[12]

Suicide, borrowing Bridges's phrase, lacerates and "wrings the human breast" like no other loss—particularly an adolescent son's or daughter's suicide. The author of Hebrews noted that Jesus "had to be made like his brothers in every way, in order that he might become a merciful and faithful high priest" (2:17) as well as to understand the palette of human experience. I have come to believe that the life and death of Judas are included in Jesus' extreme empathy. Nothing in the human experience is alien to Jesus.

The church itself has come a long way. I find comfort in the compassion demonstrated by *The Catechism of the Catholic Church*:

> We should not despair of the eternal salvation of persons who have taken their own lives. By ways known only to him alone, God can provide the opportunity for salvationary repentance. The Church prays for persons who have taken their own lives.[13]

The Book of Revelation offers a promise of a future moment: One of the elders asks, "These in white robes—who are they, and where did they come from?" He is told, "These are they who have come out of the great ordeal" (Revelation 7:13–14, Revised English Version). Kimberly Bracken Long, in a sermon at Columbia Theological Seminary, commented, "Perhaps these are the ones who have lived through more than their share of suffering, and have finally been released."[14]

If a wideness exists in God's mercy—and it does—surely that wideness includes those who have suffered and suicided, including Judas and many other of Jesus' disciples.

Reflection: Our religious cultures have often condemned those who suicide as beyond God's grace. Yet Jesus devoted his ministry on earth to revealing God's love for people who often were chastised by pious believers and religious authorities. Imagine the power of Jesus' ministry to make known God's love today, to both those who have died and those who still live.

> Prayer: Gracing God, it is so easy to demean Judas. Centuries of tradition support my disgust for this "Betrayer." Was Judas the convenient scapegoat for others who equally betrayed Jesus on his darkest night? Was Judas beyond your grace? Is my loved one? Surprise me with the wide magnificence of your mercy. Remind me of the depth of your gracious spirit. Amen.

Chapter 7

Praying Your Grief

Are you suggesting
that I pray to God
for grace "to get through"
what God could have kept
from happening?
I cannot imagine
having words to capture
and express my rage at God.

> It has always been my conviction that while there may be
> some pain that God can't explain, there is no pain that God
> can't embrace.
>
> —*William A. Ritter, whose 27-year-old son Bruce suicided*[1]

One April morning, a 7-year-old boy knelt by his bed and prayed, "Jesus, do not let anything happen to my mother." (His mother was in a hospital but the boy did not know she was in a psychiatric hospital.) That afternoon when he came home from school his father informed him that his mother had had a heart attack and had died. (His mother had slit her throat, although it would be some time before the boy learned the truth. She had been cremated while the boy and his sister were in school.) As an adult, Peter Fonda recalled the day of his mother's death: "It was Friday, April 14. Jesus had failed me. Jesus had let me down. Jesus forgot my prayer about Mother. I was too young to know that little in life was fair. . . . I never asked Jesus for anything again."[2]

"Someone's *grieving*, Lord, Kumbaya." This is my adaptation of the

African folk hymn. These words are a sung invitation to God to notice my situation, my crisis, my hopelessness, the fragileness of my faith, and my grief.

Some of the most challenging work a suicide survivor can do is to pray. To pray *fully*, survivors must bring all of themselves to the prayer: their anger, disappointment, fears, insecurities, and why's. I bring all of me into an encounter with God, aware that nothing in the human experience, or the human response to the ambushes of life, is alien to God. We can sing, "Not my brother, not my sister, but it's *me*, O Lord, standing in the need of prayer."

Some survivors pray, and some cannot or will not pray. Consider hymn-singing, a powerful mode of individual and corporate communion with God in the Christian tradition. Enya sings a joyful question, "How can I keep from singing?" Yet many survivors have difficulty singing anthems such as

> Praise to the Lord, the Almighty, the King of creation.
> O my soul, praise him, for he is thy help and salvation.
> . . . .
> Praise to the Lord, who doth prosper thy way and defend thee;
> surely his goodness and mercy shall ever attend thee;
> Ponder anew, what the Almighty can do,
> who with his love doth befriend thee.[3]

Great Sunday hymn fare may seem weak and obtuse to a survivor. How, after a suicide has thrashed your soul, can one sing, "Praise to the Lord . . . who over all things so wondrously reigneth"? Over some things, most things, yes. But *all* things? Sometimes, the best a survivor can do is to try to follow the hymn text through tear-filmed eyes.

Some lyrics irritate survivors. As Ethyl Waters sang, "His Eye Is on the Sparrow," she flashed an exuberant smile and emphasized, "And I *know* he watches *me*." Well, if his eye is on some sparrow, where was his eye focused the day my loved one suicided?

Whether by singing or by kneeling, it is often difficult for the bruised, battered, exhausted soul to pray. Joyce Rupp acknowledged this in *Praying Our Goodbyes*: "Grief has a way of plundering our prayer life, leaving us feeling immobile and empty."[4] How, drenched in anguish, do I compose words, or borrow thoughts, to direct toward a God whose ways I do not comprehend?

Two concepts are foundational in my understanding of prayer. The first I learned from Bishop John Spong in a lecture at the First United Methodist Church in Omaha in 2003: "In our prayers we roam the edges of our human experience and lift it to God without neglecting our own deepest and most personal needs."[5] Grievers approach God limping and dragging our human experience and resentments. Charlotte Elliott captured this reality in "Just as I Am" with her stanza "Fightings within and fears without, O Lamb of God I come, I come."

The second foundational concept is a German proverb: "The fewer the words, the better the prayer." Sharon, a survivor, explains her prayers after a suicide:

> I have nothing to say to God now. But I show up to see if
> he has anything to say to me. Mostly, I sit remembering this
> incredible human being who was a brief gift to me. How my
> life was blessed through this boy! And there are times, this
> will probably sound strange to some, perhaps, that I know I
> could not have summoned some of these memories. So, I have
> come to believe that God speaks to me through memories that
> wander into my mind and heart. As a mother you think, "Oh,
> I will always remember that," but memories get compressed.
> So, tell your readers to sit and wait. Remembering counts as
> prayer.

Sharon's experience is not far from the belief of Victor Hugo. "Certain thoughts are prayers. There are moments when, whatever the attitude of the body, the soul is on its knees."[6]

The Realities of Prayer

Some of the best-known words in American hymnody are these:

Have we trials and temptations,
Is there trouble anywhere?
We should never be discouraged.
Take it to the Lord in prayer.[7]

Out of great grief, Joseph Scriven wrote those words. In a way that Scriven would not have imagined, his lyrics have touched individuals around the world. He wrote them in a time of deep depression, following the deaths of his fiancées and before his own apparent suicide. Scriven understood the wisdom of taking our cares to God, yet the weight of his own troubles may have led him to end his own life.

Prayer is not easy, especially after great loss. Like Scriven, some survivors trek a trouble-strewn landscape that compounds their grief: legal issues, financial issues, insurance issues, childcare stress, family tensions, and soul fatigue. Most survivors have more on their emotional and spiritual plates than anyone could balance. Survivors wear out sentences like, "What am I going to do *about* . . . ?" or "What am I supposed to do *with* . . . ?" Lawyers, accountants, and tax advisers help with some details. Counselors offer insights, at least for some people. Yet, when suicide happens in a financially strapped or a low-income family, even basic funeral expenses can sabotage financial stability and make counseling a luxury. Even for some two-income families, suicide makes financial survival precarious. Some identify with the words of Abraham Lincoln, "I have been driven many times to my knees by the overwhelming conviction that I had nowhere else to go."[8] Yet the survivor has ample reason to respond: "Yeah, but what do I say once I am on my knees?"

Here are some points to consider:

Survivors may find prayer and praying either comforting or distressing or both.

Many grievers ask, "What do people do in times like this who do not have a faith?" Certainly, some survivors are comforted by their faith. Others, however, are frustrated by the impotence of their faith to diffuse persistent why's and the emotional demands on them, especially if there are young children or financial complications involved.

In distress, survivors may say, "I can't pray. The words will not come." Feeling blocked in prayer may lead to a frightening sense of indictment, of not having a strong enough faith. This is especially true if one is accustomed to spontaneous prayer.

To pray again, I recommend borrowing this phrase from *The Book of Common Prayer*: "Help us, in the midst of things we do not understand . . ."[9] (BCP, 862). Prayer, according to James Kimpton, "refreshes me and gives me the grace to step into the dark"—in other words, even the smallest prayer born of our confusion can guide us in the next step we must take.[10] We need not pretend to have an imperturbable faith. God will walk with us even when we can barely speak to God. Gospel songs like "Precious Lord, Take My Hand . . ." have become sung prayer for many survivors.

Difficulty praying after a suicide may become a menacing spiritual indictment.

Dwelling too long on an inability to pray may lead to distraction from the work of grief and from the mysteries of prayer. It may also cultivate an oppressive sense of guilt, of having failed God on top of all else that has gone so wrong.

The struggle to pray is not a sign of failure, but of spiritual depth. The most honest prayer may be, "O, God!" Vance Havner counseled, "If you can't pray as you want to, pray as you can. God knows what you mean."[11] In the experience of Puritan cleric John Bunyan, "The best prayers have often more groans than words."[12] Jewish philosopher Leo Rosten contends, "A place in Heaven is reserved for those who weep, but cannot pray."[13] The honesty of your cry to God speaks more eloquently than well-crafted liturgies.

Prayer may be punctuated with anger.

In Doris Grumbach's memoir, *Coming into the End Zone*, the author unleashes her anger at God. Following a young editor's death, she writes, "I am too angry with the God I trusted to save him, to lift his affliction."[14] Grumbach demonstrates that it is permissible to be angry at God. It is okay to be angry at others seemingly untouched by, or insensitive to, the raw realities of life. I know of one father who pitched condolence cards, half-read, into the trash. "I got tired of all that 'Trust God' b.s.! Like 'God never gives us more than we can handle.' I kept waiting for someone to write across the bottom of a card, 'I am as angry at God as you are.'"

Charles Williams, the trusted friend of C. S. Lewis, concluded, "If one wants to carry hot complaints to the very Throne," that is a "permitted absurdity."[15] I think it would not do violence to Williams's intent to say, "If one wants to *sling* hot complaints at the very Throne. . . ." God listens to our rage; divine wrath did not fall on Job but rather on his would-be comforters.

Praying and grief both become more complicated when friends pray for a seriously troubled loved one who then suicides.

One griever disclosed, "I prayed my guts out for my friend and he died anyway." For another survivor, the deceased seemed to be on an emotional roller coaster:

> I prayed when she was institutionalized. I prayed when she was discharged. I prayed for the psychiatrists, I prayed for the nurses, I prayed for the attendants. I prayed that this drug, or that drug, would be "the one" that would make the difference, that would give her a chance at life. I prayed that she would take her meds. Then, toward the end, when she was so like her old self, I thought, "Thank you, God, we have *finally* made it!" Two months later I buried her. Then my world fell apart.

That roller coaster may continue even after suicide. Why did God not prevent her death? Wasn't God listening when we sought help for him? The discontinuity of prayer and tragic death can make prayer seem useless and trite.

Suicide may nudge the griever to borrow prayer traditions from other expressions of spirituality.

I have suggested a particular prayer to a survivor only to be asked, "Is this a Christian prayer?" Some grievers fear anything that might be labeled "New Age," and Christianity offers rich and varied approaches to prayer. Sometimes, however, what we need comes to us from outside our usual frame of reference.

Breath Prayers: I gained awareness of breath prayers by attending an academic workshop taught by the Reverend Madeline Bastis, a Buddhist. Breathing in and out, one recites:

> May I be safe from inner and outer harm.
> May I be happy and peaceful.
> May I be strong and healthy.
> May I take care of myself with joy.[16]

You will not find these words in the current *Book of Common Prayer,* but who knows about future editions? Some of our prayers today wandered around the spiritual terrain for decades before they were deemed worthy of inclusion. So, try the first prayer:

> May I be safe [inhale]
> from inner and outer harm [exhale].

Repeat this prayer several times, inhaling on, "May I be safe . . ." and exhaling on "from inner and outer harm."

When you are ready add the second element:

> May I be happy [inhale]
> and peaceful [exhale].

Once you have become comfortable and restful with these, add this petition:

May I find good ways [inhale]
to remember my loved one's [or Name's] life [exhale].

Or:

May I come to peace [inhale]
with my loved one's [or Name's] suicide [or passing] [exhale].

Or:

May I forgive
those who failed [Name].

As you experiment with this prayer tradition, take deeper breaths. Medically, there is a great deal to commend this prayer style. Many survivors develop flu-like symptoms because, in their distress, they do not breathe deeply and the lungs are never fully emptied of carbon dioxide.

Praying in the Hebrew Tradition: Try praying a Psalm fragment while attentively breathing.

"Watch over me, God [inhale]
for I have taken refuge in you" [exhale]. (Psalm 16:1)

Change "have taken refuge" to the present tense, "For I *am taking* refuge in you."

"Watch over me, God [inhale],
for I *am taking* refuge in you" [exhale]. (Psalm 16:1)

Some survivors have discovered the rich prayer streams in Judaism. The insightful spirit of these prayers can helpfully support Jews and non-Jews alike. *Siddur Sim Shalom*, the prayer book for the Conservative Jewish movement, gives permission to remember the dead, regardless of the cause of their death. Mediate on these words:

In love we remember those who no longer walk this earth. We are grateful to God for these lives, for the joys we shared, and for the cherished memories that never fade. May God grant to those who mourn the strength to see beyond their sorrow, sustaining them despite their grief. May the faith that binds us to our loved ones be a continuing source of comfort. . . .[17]

A survivor might personalize a version of the prayer:

In love [I] remember [Name] who no longer walks this earth. God, [I am] grateful for [Name's] life, for the joys we shared, and for the cherished memories that never fade. Grant to those [of us] who mourn [Name] the strength to see beyond [our] sorrow, sustaining [us] despite [this] grief. May the faith that binds us to our loved ones be a continuing source of comfort. . . .

In Judaism mourners pray kaddish for their dead. Jews generally pray the kaddish for the first eleven months after a death. In Orthodox Judaism, praying kaddish is the responsibility of the oldest male. Kaddish must be prayed three times a day in the presence of a *minyan*—a group of ten males in Orthodox Judaism, or of ten persons in other branches of Judaism.

Glorified and sanctified be God's great name throughout the world, which He has created according to His will. May He establish His kingdom within your lifetime and within the lifetime of the whole house of Israel, speedily and soon. Amen.
    May His great name be praised unto all eternity.
    Exalted and praised, glorified and adored, extolled and revered be the name of the Holy One. Blessed is He beyond all song and psalm, beyond all praise mortal man can bestow upon him, and let us say, Amen.
    May life and abundant peace descend from heaven upon all who grieve.
    Amen.

May the Creator of heavenly peace bestow peace upon all
who grieve.
Amen.[18]

Kaddish is an important part of Jewish religious life, and it is prayed
in a prescribed way. Yet even those of us outside of Judaism and its
practices can learn from the words of the prayer. You may design a
prayer along similar lines, praising God and asking for peace "upon all
who grieve."

Prayers for the Dead: British sociologist Donald Unruh contends that
grievers need things "to do" in order to feel useful, which he calls "stra-
tegic social actions."[19] Much of the compassionate care that friends
once provided to the family of the deceased has become professional-
ized. Consequently, many grieving friends are relegated to the status
of spectators, muttering, "I just wish there were something more that
I could do."

Pray. Pray for the living who are in such distress, and pray for the
dead who is separated from you. Following the death of his friend,
the grief-sore Alfred, Lord Tennyson placed these words in the mouth
of a dying King Arthur: "If thou shouldst never see my face again,/
Pray for my soul. More things are wrought by prayer/ Than this world
dreams of."[20] Praying for the dead is difficult for some survivors, because of some Christian theological traditions. In Roman Catholicism,
however, the ancient practice of praying for the "faithfully departed"
is a long-standing tradition. Prayers for the dead permit us to say the
name of and actively remember the deceased. More importantly, when
we pray for the dead, we petition God to encompass fully the separation that has occurred through death.

Unfortunately, Martin Luther got carried away in his reforms and
dumped the tradition of praying for the dead as a "popish abomina-
tion." (Even great theologians have blind spots.) Toward the end of his
life, Luther rethought his discomfort, "The dead are still our brothers, and have not fallen from our community by death; we still remain members of a single body; therefore it is one of the duties of

'civic neighbourliness' to accompany the dead to the grave."[21] Luther instructed followers: "When you have prayed once or twice, then let it be sufficient and commend them unto God."[22] Although Luther's words underwrite our current cultural zeal for "moving along" before grief has run its full course, we can hear in his words a desire to care for those who die before us, especially by asking God to be present with them. Survivors familiar with the Anglican Catechism recognize the question, "Why do we pray for the dead?" The Anglican tradition offers this guidance: "We pray for them, because we still hold them in our love, and because we trust that in God's presence those who have chosen to serve him will grow in his love, until they see him as he is."[23]

Historically, Protestant Christians not only prayed privately for the deceased but also gathered for prayer services on the *third, ninth,* and *fortieth* days after a death as well as on the year anniversary of the death. Joyce Rupp comments that early believers knew that it would take time before a griever felt like praying or felt that prayer had any results, so friends offered prayers for the grieving, something like a spiritual proxy.[24]

It is important to recognize the church's punitive traditions regarding suicide. Christian authorities have often disenfranchised those who would pray for loved ones who took their own lives. According to this theological stance, those who committed suicide, even the baptized, went to hell immediately and were considered beyond the prayers of family and friends.

Despite the prevalence of that belief, other Christian believers, pastors, and thinkers have consistently responded with a reminder of God's all-encompassing love and desire for our prayers. John Donne, in his Christmas Day sermon in 1624, insisted, "All occasions invite his mercies and all times are his seasons!"[25]

All Souls' Day: Since the eighth century, the church has intentionally gathered to pray for the dead on All Saints' Day (November 1) and All Souls' Day (November 2). Mexican Christians pray for the dead on

Dia de los Muertos, or Day of the Dead. *The Book of Common Prayer* offers a theological underpinning for these prayers:

> Help us, God, we pray, in the midst of things we cannot understand, to believe and trust in the communion of saints, the forgiveness of sins, and and the resurrection to the life everlasting.[26]

In the mystery of the Christian faith, those who have died yet live. Unfortunately, many Christians do not appreciate the richness of an anchoring doctrine of Christianity: Christians are members of One Church made of two overlapping bodies—the Church Militant (comprised of the living) and the Church Triumphant (whose citizens are the dead). Marianne Williamson captures this reality: "The cord that binds us one to the other cannot be cut, surely not by death."[27] In the anthem "For All the Saints," we sing our theological hope—although, for some, it does not become "hope" until they have begun surviving a suicide:

> O blest communion, fellowship divine!
> We feebly struggle, they in glory shine;
> Yet all are one in Thee, for all are thine.
> Alleluia! Alleluia![28]

I am reminded, when I sing William How's lyrics, that my cousin Wilma "shines," in a way she never could as a tortured resident on earth.

Prayer does not lessen the pain of suicide—but it can change survivors.

Prayer can change our response to the demands of post-suicide life and strengthen our endurance. One powerful reality of earthquakes—and suicide is a spiritual and emotional earthquake—is *aftershocks.* The sudden loss from suicide does not end quickly, and we can expect tremors to continue to shake our lives for many years to come. Here

are prayers you might want to use or adapt as you move forward,
day by day:

> God,
> this day there is so much
> that I cannot control.
> Help me relax enough to
> trust that the necessary will be done
> and done moderately well. Amen.

> God, I offer to you
> this [name of month] day
> because I believe
> you care about how I expend my grief.
> Let me be a wise steward
> of all the opportunities
> that nudge me toward healing.
> And, by night's dawn
> may I have recognized
> your unshakeable faithfulness
> in the midst
> of all that is so unbelievable. Amen.

> God, into my life bring wise, graced individuals
>   who recognize in my pain
>   opportunities for your grace.

> God bless this day—
>   in its outrageous demands,
>   in its disguised blessings;
>   in its relentless surprises.
> Remind me, God,
>   that this is the day
>   you have created

for my good
as a survivor.
Do not, God,
let me waste my grief
this day.
Let me steward well
the hours called day,
the hours called night. Amen.

God,
the floor of my heart
is littered with questions.
Remind me today
that you understand my questions
and my questioning spirit.
Give me grace to live with the mysteries
confident of that distant day
when all will be explained. Amen.

O One
who knows me
better than I know myself
O One
who knows in my grieving season what I need
better than I can want or imagine
O One
who dreams for me
in this shattering
beyond the boundaries
of my comprehension [and imagination]
be with me
in the unfolding of this day.
Bring to me
grace sufficient
for its demands. Amen.

Pray one of these prayers—or one at the end of a chapter—as a "beachhead" to launch your conversation with God.

Grief, following a suicide, prompts some to explore a new style of prayer or to a new appreciation for prayer.

Some survivors find centering prayer meaningful. Admittedly, it takes time to get comfortable with this form of intimate prayer. The following steps can help you try this contemplative form of listening to God:

1. Sit relaxed and quiet.
2. Ask God to help you pray.
3. Select a one-syllable word, such as *peace, hope, Jesus,* Lord, *mercy,* or *grace.*
4. Turn the word over in your heart.
5. Softly repeat the word aloud.
6. When you find your mind distracted during the prayer, repeat your chosen prayer word.

Many grievers notice that their heartbeat slows and they experience a sense of calm during centering prayer. If you only have a few minutes, offer them to God. Survivors have found this a style of prayer that can be used at the first onslaught of anguish or guilt.

Finally, survivors across the centuries have found comfort in praying the Jesus Prayer. It is reminiscent of the breath prayer discussed earlier:

Lord, Jesus Christ [inhale]
Have mercy on me [exhale].

Try this ancient prayer adapted from the Sarum Prayer, a predecessor of the *Book of Common Prayer* from the fifteenth century:

GOD be in my head . . . and in my understanding as I grieve.
GOD be in my eyes . . . and in my looking as I grieve.

GOD be in my mouth . . . and in my speaking as I grieve.
GOD be in my heart . . . and in my thinking as I grieve.
GOD be at my end . . . and at my departing.[29]

Reflection: Tennyson confessed, after the death of his friend, "I some-times hold it half a sin / To put in words the grief I feel:/ For words, like Nature, half reveal / And half conceal the Soul within."[30] What in Tennyson's confession as a griever resonates with you?

Prayer: God, Faithful Presence,
   For faithfulness that exceeds my imagination.
   Thank you.
   For experiences that I do not always recognize as "blessings."
   Thank you.
   For invitations to be immersed in your grace.
   Thank you.
   For reminders of deliverance of past fears.
   Thank you.
   For grace sufficient to the demands of this day.
   Thank you.

Chapter 8

Forgiving

Forgiving is not some instant act.
For turning my world upside down,
without my permission,
I am forgiving him,
in small increments.
And some days I take back what I have forgiven.
That's the best I can do, most days.

> Sooner or later, you will need to forgive what you can't
> understand. For you may never figure it out. And even if
> you do, the conclusions you reach in your head may not
> necessarily heal what you feel in your heart. The only way
> out of your pain may be to start splashing forgiveness in
> every direction. . . .
> —*William A. Ritter*[1]

The Ernests had been friends for more than two decades. Over those
years Ernest Hotchner and Ernest Hemingway came to know each
other well. When Hotchner published his best-seller *Papa Hemingway*
after Hemingway's death, he angered the writer's widow, Mary, and
many fans by contradicting her assertion that the novelist had acci-
dentally shot himself. Hemingway had told Hotchner, "If I can't exist
on my own terms, then existence is impossible. Do you understand?
That is how I've lived and that is how I must live or not live."[2] Initially
scholars dismissed Hotchner's analysis, calling him a "celebrity seeker"
and questioning the depth of his friendship with Hemingway. Yet in

time, Mary Hemingway forgave Hotchner and acknowledged that the novelist had deliberately killed himself.

The newspaper headline caught my eye: "Victim Tells Court She Will Never Forgive." Few suicide survivors' oaths to "never forgive" become newspaper headlines, but such a vow is not uncommon. Over time, however, a promise not to forgive—whether mumbled, screamed, or voiced in the silence of the heart—is counterproductive. When such commitments are renewed periodically, unforgiveness threatens survivors' spiritual development and the integration of their loss. Take a moment and think about who you need to forgive:

The deceased?
The medical, psychiatric, or psychological community?
Those who have not "been there" for you despite their promises?
The curious, the intrusive, the insensitive?
Someone who did not take the threat to suicide seriously?
The shamers—those who inject judgment and guilt into your life, those who sabotage grace?

Many memorial services include the Lord's Prayer: "Forgive us our debts, as we forgive our debtors" (Matthew 6:12). Yet forgiveness is a continuing process, not a one-time confession. Some individuals need, from time to time, to audit their forgiveness rosters. To paraphrase a popular car ad, "Who have you forgiven *lately?*" Who needs to receive your forgiveness? On National Public Radio, I heard actor Peter Fonda reflect on his mother's death. He said that it had taken a long time to forgive her for suiciding and an even longer time to forgive his father for explaining that she had died after a heart attack.

Early in a grief, some survivors dash to forgiveness as if in a hundred-yard sprint. For most, however, forgiveness is a series of marathons in which the finish line seems to move, always disappearing over the next horizon. The pursuit of forgiveness may seem like walking a labyrinth. One often assumes, "Oh, I am almost there . . ." only to find oneself a long way from the center. Forgiveness rarely comes easily, but it is important to move toward it as an attainable goal.

Forgive the Deceased

Forgiveness may be less demanding when the deceased had a record of psychiatric unbalance. "He did not know what he was doing," we might say. But regardless of circumstances, it can be difficult to forgive when we are exhausted from asking, "Why?" Even in instances when a person's medical history significantly explains their decision to die, questions may haunt survivors for a long time to come.

Michelle Linn-Gust explained that a suicide weighs survivors down with emotional baggage. She writes, "Survivor. How I hated that word. Because my sister ended her life on her own terms, I was thrown into a category that I didn't understand, nor wanted any part of."[3] She reflected, years after her sister's suicide,

> Denise's death changed my life. And when our lives are reorganized, we must step back and reevaluate our beliefs. For me, nothing has been the same since March 18, 1992. I question everything about life more now because my sister's death took something away from me. It forced me to grow in ways I wasn't ready for.[4]

Sentimental forgiveness toward the deceased may be part of the wake and funeral. Some sense a pressure to forgive in order to "move on." Authentic forgiveness, on the other hand, is demanding. In some cases, I have suggested to mourners a forgiveness tithe: "Would you be willing to forgive ten percent with those who have hurt you, and when that is achieved will you commit to another ten percent?"

Some survivors disguise their lack of forgiveness in a world that prefers to hear, "Fine, fine. I am doing fine. Sure had it rough for a while." John, a minister, faced an incredible challenge in leading the funeral for his friend who had suicided. Initially, planning the funeral distracted him from his anger. However, he recognized that he interpreted the suicide as a rejection of his friendship. "Why couldn't you trust me when I told you that I would never abandon you?" he asked during moments alone with the corpse. After the rituals were over, the question "set in" for a protracted stay in his soul. These two friends had weathered so many crises. Why had his friend thought they would not weather this one?

Forgiveness is often painful, confusing, and lonely. Some survivors will need to forgive aspects of the deceased's life that become known only after the suicide. In *The Pilot's Wife*, Anita Shreve captures this reality starkly: "The worst is that I can't grieve. . . . How can I grieve for someone I may not even have known? Who wasn't the person I thought he was? He's gutted my memories."[5] In the light of previously unknown truths, the unfamiliarity of a loved one may cause the separation caused by their death to grow even greater.

The challenge to forgive emerges in many ways. Yet even if your memories have been "gutted," are you willing to ask God to help you extend grace to the deceased?

Forgive Yourself

Survivors find it easy to indict ourselves for a suicide. We may begin sentences with phrases such as, "If *only* I had . . ." or "I *should* have . . ." or "*Now* I realize . . . ." By the time we have rehearsed the offense we believe we have committed several times, it has swelled like cotton candy. Driving along a stretch of North Carolina interstate, I noticed a billboard that read, "Never start a sentence with 'I should have.'" That is wise advice for survivors.

Many hamstring their own healing—and the healing of others—by hogging the blame for a death. We assume so much responsibility for what happened that we fail to see the situation with any clarity at all. Adina Wrobleski and John McIntosh, in their study of 159 suicide survivors, stated that 86 percent reported having felt guilty. When the researchers followed up, almost two-thirds reported feeling guilt "for things they might have said or done but did not."[6] The weight of guilt is heavy, and it can hang on us for a long, long time.

Jim Chance, the only son of psychiatrist Sue Chance, suicided. His mother had dealt with suicide as a clinician—now she had to deal with it as a single parent.

> I lay there the night Jim died asking myself the question every survivor asks, "Why? Why, why, why, why, why, why? Let me make sense of it so I can bear it. If I can only assemble an explanation, then I can see where I failed and correct it. Maybe it won't undo this, but it'll keep me from killing anybody else with my neglect or my insensitivity or my whatever-the-hell-I-did-wrong. Better to be a monster with some hope of change than to be at the mercy of this malign randomness."[7]

She added,

> . . . I think Jim should tell me. Yes, that's right, Jim. He can come back and point a finger at me and tell me a long, long list of everything I did wrong so I can say I'm sorry and I'll do better if he'll just give me the chance. I *would* do better. I promise.[8]

It is natural to regret the loss of our loved one and to reproach ourselves for things we may or may not have done. But we must also recognize the limits of what we could have done to prevent this tragedy. Are you willing to ask God to help you extend grace to yourself?

Forgive the Medical, Psychiatric, or Psychological Community

Many survivors, according to Jann Fielden of Victoria University in New Zealand, need "to make meaning of their loved one's suicide; that is, to find a reason or plausible explanation for the suicide." This, Fielden concludes, "Appeared important in enabling survivors to move on with their grief."[9] (I would say to "move forward" in their grief.) Survivors often look to the healthcare community for scientifically grounded answers to their questions: Why did this happen? Why wasn't it preventable? Why did my loved one make this choice? However, such questions are almost always ultimately unanswerable, and some survivors blame doctors and psychiatrists for their inability to prevent their loved one's death. For example, a survivor may accuse a therapist who treated the deceased of withholding information that could lead to an explanation.

In this era of sophisticated practice, physicians, counselors, and therapists are expected to "deliver the goods" and expeditiously return the troubled to "normal," or at least some semblance of normal. Look at Jesus' encounter with the widow of Nain whose only son had died. Jesus stopped the funeral procession and "gave him back to his mother" (Luke 7:15). Likewise, many of us want sons, daughters, spouses, partners, and parents to be "given back" through the skills of mental health specialists. Instead, to some survivors who have wandered through the wilderness of psychology, psychiatry, medicine, and insurance with a suffering relative or friend, engaging health professionals after a suicide feels like an endless funeral procession.

In today's atmosphere of "better living through pharmaceuticals," many of us are unrealistically encouraged by the "latest" pharmaceutical or for the arrival of a new clinician, especially when there are reports "that he has done wonders with" a particular person, procedure, or chemical combination. After a suicide, initial interactions with health and psychological professionals may create "intense feelings of hurt and anger in survivors."[10] Hope of significant permanent change has been dashed on the permanence of death. The promise of a healed life that we understood modern medicine to hold failed our loved one in the end, and it continues to fail us by not even being able to explain the death that has occurred.

When physicians and mental health professionals disappoint or fail to meet expectations, real or unstated, too many survivors march their frustrations to a lawyer's office and into a courtroom. An element in medical malpractice suits is sometimes a lack of forgiveness for the failure of health professionals to save a loved one. Other survivors, however, will not sue. Instead, they badmouth that clinician or the entire mental health establishment. Sometimes, annoyance turns into anger by the perception of a lack of sufficient postmortem concern expressed by the clinician, particularly when she claims doctor-client confidentiality or explains that she is being monitored by attorneys anxious to avoid litigation. No few survivors nurture resentment towards the healthcare community that takes up more and more emotional and spiritual space. Some insist, "I have a right to feel the way I do!" Perhaps, but what cost does the expression of that right exact?

Survivors have laid claim to justice—and monetary compensation— to grant absolution to the clinician who is made painfully naked by the suicide. But let us think more broadly: Who listens to the grieving clinician whose patient suicided? Imagine the mental anguish of the doctor who wonders if survivors will sue? In fact, psychologist and suicide specialist Jack Jordan identifies clinicians as survivors.[11] Having walked with two clinician-friends through the minefield of litigation, I know its paralyzing impact.

Admittedly, the defensive posturing of clinicians insults survivors. Yet if we take the time to think about everyone affected by this loss, we may audit our attitudes toward the "helpers" who did not help sufficiently. An attorney's office should not be the first stop after the memorial service. Indeed, some survivors find the path to their own healing only after offering the palm branch of grace to a doctor some would say failed. Are you willing to ask God to help you extend grace to the medical, psychiatric, or psychological community?

Forgive Those Who Have Not "Been There" for You

Most postmortem promises have a short shelf life. When friends assert their readiness to help after a death, their statements of support usually come with invisible expiration dates. One angry survivor demanded, "Where are the people who made all the promises?"

The infrequency with which acquaintances actually make good on their pledges of support may have something to do with our tendency to avoid pain at almost all costs. Anne Lamott considers these vows to lend a hand as "exit lines," ways to extract ourselves from uncomfortable conversations soon after a death. Fear of our own vulnerability to be hurt may explain how some would-be supporters behave. When some individuals look at survivors, they may not see the individual; they may see the pain experienced by that person. They see mirrored in the survivor their own fear. "My god!" they may think. "This could happen to me!"

It is also difficult for those less intimately tied to a death to understand the time grief demands of us. Anne Lamott reflects, "In Jesus' real life, the resurrection came two days later, but in our real lives, it can be weeks, years, and you never know for sure that it will come."[12] It is not that people do not mean the offers they make. Rather, they may not expect you to "cash the coupon," even after only a short time has passed.

Regardless of reasons, the failure of friends to support us only deepens our own troubles. Finding the resources to forgive those we love who have disappointed us in our time of need may take a long time and much work. Are you willing to ask God to help you extend grace to those who have not been there for you?

Forgive the Curious, the Intrusive, the Insensitive

Some individuals ask intrusive questions in order to assess your eligibility for receiving their compassion, probing into your feelings and hurt for their own benefit. As the saying goes, "Inquiring minds want to know." For them, if you say, "My son had been under medical treatment for depression for some time . . . ," you can see the "Aha . . ." forming in their minds. The patronizing indecency of this kind of prying can hurt deeply. Sometimes not their question but their tone of voice lacerates the mourner. Or their embarrassed pause. Some of these hurtful encounters are "time-released": they can sting for hours or days after they occur.

Thankfully, these kinds of judgments are much milder than the treatment once commonly received by survivors of suicide. Few grievers today hear, "Well, it's obvious that she is not in heaven!," a judgment once common following suicide. Historically, the deceased—and indirectly their families—were denied full liturgical rites and burial in consecrated soil. Corpses were degraded by being hung upside down or dragged through the streets. Some had stakes driven through their hearts. Others were buried at the edge of cemeteries rather than in family plots. This lack of ritual grace was a double insult to the soul, compounding the already excruciating pain of dealing with a loved one's choice to die.[13]

Still today, however, some would-be comforters play theologian. These intruders may bluntly wield scripture—*their* interpretation of scripture—to support their judgment. Recently, my heart has gone out to the families whose loved ones' funeral services have been sabotaged by protesters from the Westboro Baptist Church and the Reverend Fred Phelps of Wichita, Kansas. On June 20, 2005, Phelps's followers picketed the funeral of Sgt. Casey Byers, recently killed in Iraq—unaware that his brother, Army Spc. Justin "Paul" Byers, had committed suicide after learning of his brother's death and his own deployment to Iraq. Under free speech, local police protected the picketers (and their outrageous inflammatory signs). When questioned by a reporter, Abigail Phelps, lead picketer, retorted:

> I was not aware of that [the son's suicide], and if that is the case then I am wondering what great evil those parents have been engaged in that God would render this one, two punch. . . . I advised her of the true nature of the Sovereignty of God and our duty to be thankful for each of His works, period.

Ms. Phelps told a reporter that were she the soldiers' parents, she would find the "darkest, deepest closet to go hide in, and get on my knees . . . [and] beg for God's forgiveness, and to please spare me from the doom I most surely deserve."[14]

Thoughtful care does not flow generously through the souls of some believers. There are "compassion challenged" people on the loose in the Kingdom of God. Among those who hurt you, you may need to forgive those whose comments have been "reported" to you second-hand. Their judgments may have become warped in repetition, or they may have leveled their convictions just as you hear them. You will probably never know, and such rumors will almost certainly cause you pain whether true or not.

If you can, consider that most have never experienced what you are experiencing—even those who have had deaths to grieve. They are clueless about the rolling carnage that a suicide creates.

If it is difficult for you to forgive, pray Jesus' words: "Father, forgive them for they do not know what they are [saying]" (Luke 23:34). You may need to preface this prayer with a petition for grace to forgive. "God bring me to the point where I can forgive . . ."

Take a moment to sit in silence. Let a face or name come to you—someone who has hurt you. Pray, "Father, [name] has hurt me by . . . . Help me forgive [name]." You might add, "Help me to see [name] as you see him/her." In reality, if the suicide happened a long time ago, survivors may have to first thaw the issue out in order to recognize the wound inflicted on them fully and thereby forgive the other person adequately.

Soul-stretching forgiveness comes only in partnership with God. In order to forgive someone who has deeply hurt them, some survivors come, in time, to a new perception of the forgiveness they have, over time, received. Are you willing to ask God to help you extend grace to the curious, the intrusive, and the insensitive?

Forgive Those Impatient with the Grief Integration Process

Some acquaintances of the grieving sound like impatient kids on vacation. "Aren't we there yet?" they complain. These comments can intimidate survivors. "Aren't you over it *yet?*" shows little sympathetic consideration. Albert Hsu, after his father's suicide, concluded: "We are never completely healed. After all, we still carry the scars. But grief that has done its work in us will help us experience God's grace more fully."[15]

Some wounds will not be completely healed until eternity's dawn. Only God's kingdom has resources sufficient to achieve the healing we need.

Many onlookers—some friends and even family members—will be impatient for you to get "closure." They want to see the "proof" that you have moved on. Several friends told Joan Rivers following her husband's death, "We want the old Joan back." She responded, "Never let others bully you out of your particular style" of grieving.[16] Rivers was clear with others that the "old Joan" no longer existed. Hsu captures the spiritual paradox that emerges as grief extends over time. "I did not find 'closure,'" he writes. "But I experienced God's closeness."[17]

Are you willing to ask God to help you extend grace to those who are impatient with the grief integration process?

Forgive the Grace Saboteurs

Grace scares the hell out of a lot of Christians. Some sputter when I say the act of suicide is no barrier to heaven. "What!? But the Bible says . . ." Some volunteer to be gatekeepers, "bouncers," to keep the "riff-raff" out of the celestial city. I can almost see them in heaven grabbing someone and snarling, "Hey, what are you doing here? You committed suicide! You're supposed to be in *hell*." Some individuals will have a hard time enjoying heaven once the wideness of God's mercy confronts them. Some have missed out on the good news that suicide is not a spiritual equivalent of "Go directly to jail. Do not pass go. Do not collect $200." But worse than their disappointment at the openness of God's heavenly home, many have missed opportunities to be trench buddies with survivors because of their theological bias.

So, what about hell and the belief held by some Christians, that suicide cannot be forgiven? Albert Hsu submits one view:

Christians do not hold the false hope that all who die regardless of faith will go to heaven. We take Jesus seriously when he says that there are two paths, one to life and another to destruction, and people will wind up in one of two eternal destinies. . . . We take seriously the reality that there is a heaven and a hell, and all of us will someday see one or the other.[18]

On the other hand, I appreciate the assessment in an editorial entitled "Do We Still Need Hell?" which appeared in *The Christian Century*: "God, like the father of the Prodigal Son, will never turn out the lights on us, will never assume we are beyond redemption."[19] From this perspective the love of God encompasses all of our choices.

The Christian burial service is called the committal because survivors commit the body to the earth, water, or fire and the soul to God—a God merciful beyond our wildest imagination. A God who "devises ways so that the banished do not remain estranged from him forever" (2 Samuel 14:14).

Unfortunately, theological gatekeepers miss opportunities to be co-comforters with our all-merciful God. Someone once asked ethicist Lewis Smedes, "Is suicide unforgivable?" based on the premise that a person who suicides could not have repented of their final act. Smedes thoughtfully reminded the questioner, "We all die with sins not named and repented of." Smedes then expanded on his answer:

Will Jesus welcome home a believer who died at her own hands? I believe he will, tenderly and lovingly. My biblical basis? It is the hope-giving promise of Romans 8:38, that neither life nor death can separate the believer from the love of God in Christ Jesus.[20]

There is no asterisk in that verse, no exception saying, "*Except* for suicide." Are you willing to ask God to help you extend grace to the grace saboteurs?

Forgive the World

It takes only moments for survivors to realize that while your world has been irrevocably shattered, "the" world goes on. Michelle Linn-Gust remembers,

> Nothing stopped after Denise died. As we drove to her funeral, cars passed us en route to jobs or errands. . . . I always thought the cruelest part of Denise's death was that the world didn't stop to acknowledge she was no longer with us.[21]

The busy routine of the world can seem irreverent and absurd when we have stopped to grieve a death. But the world will go on, and we must cope with its ignorance of our suffering. Are you willing to ask God to help you extend grace to the world that refuses to stop after anyone's suicide?

Reflection: Do yourself a favor: Make space in your grieving to give attention to forgiveness.

> Prayer: Eternal Forgiver, you are aware of my reluctance to forgive, my desire to believe that I have some right not to forgive the one who initiated my grief and those who have complicated my grief. Stir recognition in my heart of the need to forgive. Remind me of how generously you have forgiven me. Give me sufficient courage to forgive lavishly and thoroughly. Amen.

Chapter 9

Investing in a Charitable Narrative

The long hard work begins.
I have to balance these "last memories"
—the things I have discovered
about someone I thought I knew
with old memories.
I want to remember to remember
the life not the death.
I want to remember to remember to be charitable
and to offer the good memories hospitality
so that they will become permanent residents in my heart.

> [Account making is] the way we spontaneously seek op-
> portunities to tell and retell the stories of our loss, and in
> so doing, recruit social validation for the changed stories
> of our lives.
>   —*Robert Neimeyer*[1]

Suicide happens while those who will survive are making other plans. John Quincy Adams's defeat for a second term as president by Andrew Jackson in 1829 was an enormous humiliation to him. His family was in tatters. Choosing to live in the capital, the former president summoned George, 28, his oldest son, to Washington for a confrontation on his "scandal-ridden, dissolute life." Traveling by steamer, George, an alcoholic who battled depression, jumped overboard to his death. After John Quincy Adams II was expelled from Harvard for behavior unbecoming a gentleman, he became his father's private secretary.

Unfortunately, alcoholism impaired his judgment and service. John II died in 1834 at age 31. This distraught former President groaned, "No one knows the agonies I suffered."[2] Many survivors have expressed the same thought.

For some, a charitable memory is preferable to last memories of heated discussions, fights, slammed doors, harsh, ugly, unforgettable words slung in anger or desperation. Or discoveries after a death that shattered the perception of a person, of a relationship with them.

Other survivors have been traumatized by finding the loved one dying, or by finding the corpse. One mother groaned, "It's hard to forget finding the brain that aced the SAT splattered all over inside of the family car. How do I forget that?"

Choosing Memories

Survivors must create a charitable narrative by sorting through memories. Patti Davis compared this to shuffling cards.

> Throughout our lives, we shuffle images in our memories— as if they were a deck of cards or, more accurately, a stack of photographs. One picture ends up on top, face up, an emblem of what we have chosen to remember. We do it with places, with events, but most often we do it with people. The image we choose varies according to where we are in our lives, who we have become, how generous or angry or philosophical we are about the person we are trying to remember.[3]

We have a variety of memories; to a certain extent, we can try to select those that help us continue our own lives as survivors. Challenging us to reexamine our memories, Edwin Shneidman asks, "Is it possible for you to see the past in a slightly different way?"[4] The survivor, in order to make the unbearable potentially bearable, must reexamine the past shared with the deceased.

I occasionally lead survivors in an exercise in which we say, "I must remember to remember. . . ." The survivors audit their relationship with the deceased to identify important elements they do not want to forget. The second part of the exercise is, "I must remember *to forget.* . . ." Troublesome memories arrive unbidden on the front screens of the mind with the intensity of a child determined to gain a parent's attention. While suppressing these thoughts is not helpful, survivors can nevertheless choose "to watch the thoughts go by as if we were watching a parade."[5] Let the memory "go by"—notice it, but do not hit the "replay" button. We can remember without grasping hold of these difficult thoughts. We can let them go. Healthy survivors do not offer hospitality to negative thoughts and memories.

A Charitable Memory Requires Safe Spaces

Survivors need a safe place to acknowledge and grieve the real relationship they have with the person who has died. Within the traditions of Orthodox Judaism is this warning, "Cursed be anyone who says 'Amen,' to a false eulogy." It is important to remember our loved ones with honesty. To do that, we need to take the time to consider our memories and to choose wisely which ones we hold nearest our hearts. We need a safe space in which we can confront this death with honesty.

Creating a charitable memory is essential to integrating the loss we have suffered, because a charitable memory helps us continue to live in relationship with the one we have lost. But this takes work. A survivor does not simply "erase" or record over existing memories as one would reuse a videocassette. One cannot wipe the hard drive clean. Difficult, frightening, and disillusioning memories may remain embedded within us like land mines for a long, long time. Humans have no "delete" key in the mind or heart to rid themselves of what we don't want to remember. Yet with time and our careful cooperation, some memories can soften around the edges or fade in intensity, like old photographs.

The complexity of our relationship with the one who has died before their death can make charitable remembering even harder. In *Liberating Losses: When Death Brings Relief*, Jennifer Elison and Chris

McGonigle contend that not every partner, relative, or friend of the deceased was a "loved one" at the time of death. Marilyn Hauser notes that suicides often occur in families that have experienced considerable stress, strain, and dysfunction. Those patterns of behavior often continue among survivors after a suicide. Blame, fruitless fighting, and unexpressed anger can make arriving at a true and livable memory of the one who has died difficult.

> . . . the process of blaming tends to isolate the family and to promote emotional rifts within. Ultimately, the selective communication and cut-offs lead to the formation of distorted fantasies and beliefs about the deceased and the family. Out of these fantasies family myths and secrets are born, further impeding relationships within and outside the family.[6]

Without honesty, the hard work of grief becomes harder through distortion. It has to be the real you grieving the real deceased. Yet family dynamics can complicate each survivor's ability to remember the dead. Conflict may arise between competing "voices" within a family's constellation of grief. In some families, the loudest narrative drowns out others. Karen recounts her experience at her grandfather's memorial service:

> I did not recognize my grandfather in the eulogy. I listened to the minister describe him as a "model" Christian, father, grandfather, and as a pillar of the community. What I remembered were his whisperings, "Honey, Grandpa needs a little sugar." I remembered his fingers inside my dress, inside my panties. And his constant reminder, "This is our little secret, darling? You're granddaddy's favorite."

Surviving her grandfather's suicide was challenged by a cognitive dissonance between the real memories Karen had and what she thought she was supposed to acknowledge as acceptable memories. A survivor may feel isolated if she or he assumes molestation occurred only to himself or herself. It takes courage to voice one's truth: "He molested me."

That statement will send a family into convulsions, but that expressed courage may free another family member also to say, "I thought *I* was the only one." The family may then fight to limit the fissure of this new knowledge before it runs through the whole family narrative. Occasionally, when a threatened disclosure of abuse or wrongdoing preceded a suicide, family members may turn against the discloser. "*You* drove him to this!" they may accuse. In the emotional confusion, a survivor may assume guilt that does not belong to them. But that is not the truth. No: Choices the deceased made motivated the suicidal decision.

A Charitable Memory Takes Energy

Memory-reorganizing can be demanding emotional and spiritual work. Grief has a way of challenging all our commitments and priorities. Imagine a cue ball smacking a rack of billiard balls. The impact sends balls careening around the table, not just the ball that took the impact.

It demands great emotional and spiritual energy to "maintain" a dissonant memory, or to reconcile a newly edited narrative with an existing version. Lots of grievers feel exhausted by the effort, drained. We need energy, and opportunities to renew our energy, in order to grieve our loss.

Even After Time Has Passed, a Charitable Memory May Remain Incomplete

After the suicide of Denny, a college companion of Calvin Trillin's, friends gathered together to spend time reconciling their memories of earlier years with the latest version of Denny's life, the one they heard at his funeral service. Reflecting on that time, Trillin developed a charitable memory of his friend in his memoir *Remembering Denny*. Yet, years after the death, he mused,

Still, I don't know why Denny killed himself. After all these
years of poking around in other people's lives, I'm convinced
that we can almost never know the precise motives of someone
else, even old friends.[7]

Trillin sought to understand his friend's life and death in many ways,
through conversations, self-reflection, and writing. The work of building a charitable memory of Denny required many years, and questions
remained unresolved. Some significant details of a life—or periods of a
life—are not accessible to a eulogist, or even to family members.

Acknowledgment of the complexity of a life is one of the "gifts" of
funerary rites, particularly the visitation or wake. While the memorial service is generally ritual- or liturgy-focused (and, in many cases,
time-constrained), the visitation is narrative-focused and more infor-
mal. Some individuals make their way to a visitation with an agenda:
"I have a story to tell you about [Name]," they may say. Occasionally,
the narrative shared is unknown, unsuspected, by family members.
Few of us know the full extent of the relationships of a family member,
friend, or colleague; sometimes, long after a death, individuals come
forward to offer memories to amend or expand the narrative we have
constructed.

The inevitable incompleteness of our understanding of the one
who has died can fall victim to those who would use this death for
their own purposes. Yet constructing a charitable memory of the dead
can withstand the hurt inflicted by others. Admiral Jeremy Michael
Boorda, chief of staff of the United States Navy, suicided in 1996.
Boorda's critics drew attention to the Admiral's Vietnam service medal.
In their judgment, he was not entitled to wear it. Yet in the funeral service at the National Cathedral, President Clinton masterfully created
a charitable memory for the family and the many friends and mourners of Boorda. "Even though he was very small [in stature], the rest
of us always looked up to him, looked up to his ability to inspire us
all to do better, to reach beyond ourselves." Clinton highlighted the
Admiral's interactions with enlisted sailors and praised the Admiral's
peacemaking in the Balkans and the Dayton Accords:

I very much want history to record that Mike Boorda's quiet determination to do all we could do to end the slaughter of the children and the innocents in Bosnia and to bring that awful war to an end had a profound impact on his President and on the policy of this Nation. . . . And there are countless thousands of people alive in Bosnia today because of this small man with a big heart, a large vision, and great courage.

The President concluded his remarks:

Now Mike Boorda's ship is moored. His voyage is complete. But I know when the whistle blew and the colors were shifted he was welcomed on the pier by God's loving eternal embrace. May God bless and cherish Admiral Mike Boorda as he blessed and cherished our lives and our beloved America.[8]

In contrast to these words was the public attention focused on Boorda's death. Unfortunately, the Boorda family had to do their initial griefwork in the eye of the public and a hyperactive media. "Inquiring minds want to know. . . ," we are too often reminded. Pundits were drooling for another Vincent Foster episode to stir up ratings and raise funds for right-wing causes. The suicide of a good man provided fresh meat for Clinton-critics and the media, who immediately found talking heads to fill up airtime with speculation and psychobabble. To hell with the grieving family's right to privacy, such behavior seemed to say. But in the heat of public scrutiny, one thing could not be denied: The President created a charitable memory for the family and friends at the memorial service for Admiral Jeremy Michael Boorda.

A Charitable Memory Takes Courage

For some survivors, going through the details and possessions of a life looking for clues from which to build a memory is draining. Survivors may find things they do not want to know or see. When Anthony suicided in New Orleans, his estranged family in Kentucky wanted an immediate cremation and no ritual. A sister drove down to retrieve his belongings. A procession of Anthony's friends made their way to his apartment to offer her condolences—and to bear stories, slices of memory. While she found images and snapshots of her brother in activities that she would prefer not to have seen, in the scales of memory the balance swung to a dimension of Anthony that she had not known. She found herself comforting his friends. On the spur of the moment, his friends threw a non-traditional "going away" party for Anthony. Some of the eulogies "challenged" this farm woman from Kentucky— two male friends showing up in full drag—but the tenor of the salute changed her experience. She was stunned by the recitation of the emotional and financial care Anthony had provided friends—especially those who also had AIDS.

She has kept up with some of his friends in phone conversations, email, and postcards. A few friends have found their way to her kitchen table in Kentucky. Especially on Halloween, Anthony's favorite holiday, and on the anniversary of his death, she sits with charitable memories of her brother. Like a photograph enlarged on a computer, her charitable memory has been expanded through a wider awareness of her brother's life.

A Charitable Memory Requires Support

Few survivors can do charitable memory work alone. Grief group work can be advantageous and can stimulate spiritual and personal integration of the loss. Iris Bolton describes her experience in a group:

> We continued to meet regularly for we had found a place where we could talk freely and express our deepest feelings. It was a revelation to listen to people who had mourned a death for years, thinking all the while that they were slightly crazy, or at the very least, peculiar and spineless. . . . The good that came out of it was that through talking to each other we discovered that we were normal, lonely human beings who had

been temporarily stuck in the traffic jam of perpetual grieving. By being with each other we were able to work our way free.[9]

I lead "mutual-help" groups, which work like a psychological pot-luck. Everyone contributes to the "meal." I act as facilitator, but not as a grief expert. Our group's symbol is a ceramic statue of individuals warming themselves around a fire, arms wrapped around each other's shoulders. Mutual-help grief groups support survivors to discover that they are not alone and that the story of another griever may contain resources for their healing. Mutual-help groups offer survivors safe places to express feelings honestly. They enfranchise stories that have been repressed and shamed. Mutual-help groups offer places to acknowledge the peculiarities of our grief journeys.[10] Some individuals launch significant memory-making work with a clinical social worker, pastor, chaplain, psychologist, or psychiatrist. Over time, as trust is built in the relationship, the mourner's narrative is reexamined, amended, or rewritten. Unfortunately, some survivors have learned painfully that not every professional "helper" can guide effective grief navigation following a suicide. Then the survivor must renew the search for a therapist who can.

Hesped

Over the years, I have borrowed and developed spiritual exercises from many religious traditions that facilitate the development of a charitable memory. I have long believed in the adage, "something old, something new, something borrowed, something *true*." Our own spiritual tradition may not be a sufficiently deep "pool" to provide resources to meet our needs as survivors. So, we must borrow from other people, from other places.

One rich gift I have found in Judaism is *hesped*, or a eulogy. Such a memorial traditionally praises the life of the person who has died, commending them to God by remembering their good deeds. From this practice we can derive a more general *hesped*, a balanced eulogy that helps us remember the fullness of a person in honesty and with charity toward them. You can offer a balanced eulogy through an activity like this: Take a sheet of paper and list the alphabet down the left side—a, b, c, through to z. Beside each letter of the alphabet list a positive and a negative characteristic of the deceased that begin with that letter. For example, *approachable* or *always there for me* and *arrogant* or *absent*.

The purpose of a balanced eulogy is to help us honestly remember the person who has died as a full human being, flawed and praiseworthy. The picture this eulogy creates of the deceased can move us closer to constructing a charitable memory of them. Sometimes we may desire support in this, especially when our perspective on the person begins to seem too slanted toward positives or negatives. To do this exercise, some participants may wish to talk with family members, friends, and work colleagues in order to enlarge their circle of memory through dialogue. Other people's memories of the deceased can be very helpful, because occasionally participants in a balanced eulogy are hamstrung by the cultural injunction, "Speak no ill of the dead." Yet when it is done honestly, most participants gain a clearer balance in their memories through this variation on the Jewish practice of *hesped*.

Reflected Eulogy

Many eulogies are constructed and delivered under some element of time pressure—either in preparing or in delivering the eulogy. Unfortunately, some families take a "get it over with as quickly as possible" stance when it comes to memorial services. But the result of hurrying ourselves through grief is too often what we might call "ritual lite"—the substance of funeral rituals, which can help us accept the reality of death and engage the grieving process, is lost in the desire to avoid the real pain of laying the deceased to rest. Eulogies, like other elements of a service, deserve as much of our attention as we can give them.

Yet how do you summarize a life in a few minutes? How many

eulogies have begun, "Where do I begin to talk about [Name] . . . ?" Or, "There are so many things I could say about [Name]." When the person we are remembering has suicided, a eulogy may seem even more difficult to deliver. Often no one wants the cause of death mentioned at all, especially not in the eulogy. At some funeral or memorial gatherings, suicide is the unspoken presence in the room. Everyone knows the manner of death, but no one acknowledges it. "Whatever you do, do not mention the 's' word!" some might pray under their breath. In some cases, individuals sit in anxious silence, hoping the eulogist will not stray into controversial acknowledgments of how this person died. Indeed, we might all agree that at a memorial service, certain things are best left unsaid.

In our mutual-help groups, I ask survivors to write a three-page biography of their deceased, including things that did not get said—or could not be said—in the formal eulogy or the obituary. Some read these biographies as if trying to beat an imaginary buzzer; others "unravel" the narrative like a meandering drive down a country road. Some biographies are punctuated with laughter by the participant and by the group; others are punctuated by tears and, occasionally, flashes of anger. Often survivors regret that, in the rush of activity after a death, important things went unstated or remained *under*stated. Every life is full of complexity, and it is worth finding a way to tell the story of our loved one's life in greater detail and in a public setting. A funeral eulogy can be only the beginning of how we speak about those who have died.

In essence, this exercise—to write a biography of the one who has died and to read their story to willing listeners—gives us another opportunity say what we feel needs to be said in memory of the person who has died.

Anniversaries

The anniversary of a suicide is a significant date on the calendar of the heart. It is spiritually wise to recognize the anniversary rather than dodge it; avoiding the day will often only plant within you a feeling of unease and sorrow. Remembering the day of this death will almost certainly be deeply painful, and friends may want to spare you that grief. Survivors have to ignore the attempts of those who would intentionally distract from honoring the anniversary of a suicide in order to face the day squarely. You may ask yourself, "What can this anniversary teach me?"

In Judaism, while the first anniversary of a death is especially important because it is the time for the unveiling of the grave marker, each anniversary invites intentional acknowledgment. People of the Jewish faith name the anniversary *yahrzeit* (meaning "time of year" in Yiddish). We may learn the importance of remembering the dead through the witness of the Jewish community.

Outside of Judaism, some survivors will grudgingly "go along" with noting a first anniversary but resist honoring future anniversaries. "We need to move on!" they protest, and so they miss the opportunity for the anniversary of a death to be a significant spiritual experience. A yearly ritual is a way to "continue to hold onto what was precious to us," the person who has died.[11]

Make the most of an anniversary. Use a day of personal leave to step out of your daily routine and focus on what has come to pass. Find ways to remember the one who has died. Leaf through or reorganize photograph albums. Listen to the deceased's favorite music. Go to a special place or restaurant. Visit the grave or scattering area of the person who has died. One survivor, whose brother is buried hundreds of miles away, scanned pictures of his grave onto her laptop. Periodically, she "goes" to the cyber grave and remembers him.

You can write a *yahrzeit* poem, an anniversary essay, or a yearly prayer. If helpful, you might use this phrase to jumpstart your creativity: "On this day, etched permanently on my heart, I . . . ." Or you can adapt this phrase to begin, "Another year has passed . . . ."

> Another year has passed.
> Another year with hundreds
> of times thinking,
> "I should tell [Name] about . . . ."

Life is about making a place
for our griefs,
for our missing moments.
But life is also about living
in anticipation of that morning,
however soon or distant,
when Gabriel will sound his sweet trumpet
and the dead shall rise!
[Name], I am thinking of you this day.

Some may protest, "But I want to forget [or I want another person who is grieving to forget] the date!" You are not going to forget. It will be, or already is, chiseled into the lining of your heart. So, why not embrace the anniversary creatively and spiritually? By unapologetically honoring the anniversary, you model a healthy spiritual attitude, and you give others "permission" to honor their loved one's *yahrzeit.*

Visiting the Grave or Scattering Area

For some survivors, creating a narrative of the deceased's life is a work-in-process, work done in increments. I encourage individuals to read words, prayers, or poems they have written about the deceased and the suicide at that person's grave or scattering point. Honor their life. Trust your emotions. Create and release what you feel.

Sometimes, truth gets "told" at a cemetery in an important way. Iris Bolton describes an "anger release" at her son's grave.

I went to my son's grave one afternoon and demanded of the
air and the sky and of God himself that they tell me what right
my son had to leave me in such pain, to defile my life, to have
refused my efforts to help. Finally, my anger burned itself out.
It was over, like a plunge across an icy pool.[12]

At other times, a survivor says at a marker, "This is what I want to always remember about [Name]. . . ." It may do more "good" for the survivor to verbally unload at a grave rather than let the accusations they feel career inside their souls like bumper cars. Some survivors come to cemeteries because it is the only place they feel comfortable disclosing their hearts. Maria comes occasionally on her lunch break to her brother's grave; she even occasionally brings his favorite seasonal snacks to leave at the tomb. Time passes, and there are still things she wants to say and share with her brother.

Stories need to escape the heart. As I wander by grave markers, I sometimes pause to ask, "Who were you?" Or "Who could you have become if you could have glimpsed the future?" The graves of the young who gave up on their lives trouble me. One young man hung himself because he thought his friends would abandon him, as had his family, when they discovered that he was gay. All the hiding wore out his heart and his ability to imagine surviving the present until he could live out a future in a place far from Kansas City. What joy he might have brought to someone. What a difference he might have made in the workplace—in a lab, or a parish, or a studio, or an office. What contributions might he have made to a community if he could have lived long enough to comprehend his right to honor himself.

Some graves have no hint of explanation. "Still as big a mystery to me," one widow explained, "as the day he pulled the trigger."

> I have worn out all my why's. My priest says I just have to live without a good explanation. Jose loved his garden, and the yard work. He cut the grass one Saturday afternoon, went out to the garage to put away the lawnmower and shot himself. No note, no warning, no goodbye. So, I stop by to make sure his grave is tidy. It is my gift to him.

Charitable Gifts Build Charitable Memories

Survivors create charitable memories by continuing acts of mercy, justice, or righteousness that were important to the deceased. Investing in a cause valued by the one who has died is a way for their actions in life to continue bearing fruit. A charity loses a donor with a death, although there may be initial memorial gifts. Honor your deceased's favorite organization with donations—the size of the contribution is unimportant—on birthdays, holidays, or on the *yahrzeit*.

> There are places in my heart
> on certain days
> no other memories will do.
> So, I resurrect him, out of sight.

Fortunately for today's new survivors, there has been a relative de-stigmatization of suicide. In a way quite different than in the past, it is possible to make public acts in the name of a person who suicided. You can contribute to that reality by determining that remaining stigmas will not silence you. Iris Bolton, for example, has broken the silence surrounding suicide through lecturing at conferences and through writing her book, *My Son . . . My Son*. What might you do? It may be as simple as sponsoring the altar flowers or candles for the Sunday closest to the anniversary of your loved one's death. This is a way to keep the deceased before the congregation. In such ways, you can invite others to openly value the memory of the one who has died.

All Souls' Day

In liturgical churches, All Souls' Day offers an opportunity to commemorate the dead. If you are part of a faith community that does not celebrate All Souls', devise your own All Souls' Day remembrance with a special prayer, reflective time, meal, or gathering of family members. You can sing the hymn, "For All the Saints Who from Their Labors Rest." Read and reflect upon the lyrics and upon the life of your loved one, your life together, and on your life as a survivor. Offer a prayer of gratitude that you have survived—are surviving—what you thought unsurvivable. If you like, adopt the tradition from Judaism of lighting a *yahrzeit* candle. (This candle is traditionally lit on the evening before the anniversary of the death and burns for a full twenty-four hours. The flame represents the soul of the departed, because the "human spirit is the lamp of the Lord" [Proverbs 20:27].) Visit the grave or scattering area. Give memory intentional space.

Charitable Memories

Shakespeare wrote, "Give sorrow words." Let us "give memory words." Free your memories! Deborah Coryell urges, "Say what is in your heart and if there are no words, trust the silence. Do what is in your heart and if there is nothing to do, do nothing with your eyes open."[13]

Give yourself permission to make a charitable memory. Iris Bolton's family went out to dinner to "honor" her son's death day. When Iris lifted her glass to propose a toast "to Mitch," his brother Bob was startled. "To Mitch?" he asked.

"Yes, to his *life* and to the good times," Iris responded. Bob broke into a smile, "Yes, here's to his *life*."[14]

Reflection: Creating a charitable memory helps survivors "reestablish a new life worthy of passionate reinvestment."[15] Creating a charitable memory stretches the soul and leads you to a precinct of peace. What can you do, today, to build a charitable memory of the person who has died?

> Prayer: Rememberer, I am determined to do my part to honor the life of [Name]. If he/she has not been forgotten by you, he/she should not be forgotten by me. Give me courage to create ways to mark the blessings of his/her life and to ignore the protests of those who do not understand. Amen.

Chapter 10

Futuring

I cannot imagine
any future worth having
without [Name].
I want back what I had
not some consolation prize.

> In the wake of bereavement, then, we are forced to re-
> negotiate our identity as a survivor in interaction with
> others, seeking an audience that will validate the new ver-
> sion of self we enact. This process . . . [entails] a search for
> that which remains viable in our previous lives and an in-
> vention of new roles and ways of being that are appropriate
> to our changed worlds.
> —*Robert A. Neimeyer*[1]

In those first hours after finding her husband dead of a gunshot wound on the bathroom floor, could Katharine Graham have imagined that in the future she would turn a second-rate newspaper into a national media powerhouse, influence the resignation of a president, or write a best-seller? Until 1963 she had been a housewife, a mother of four children, married to a philandering manic-depressive husband. Then her husband suicided, leaving her alone with children to care for and choices to make. After a period of reflection on her future, she returned to take the helm of the family business. One individual remembered, "Men in suits thought they would be able to wrest the company from someone so crippled with anxiety that she practiced saying, 'Merry

Christmas' before giving her first staff party." There must have been people at that party who boasted, "I give her six months, at best. . . ." But as a biographer noted: "She was a brainy graduate of the University of Chicago with common sense who hired good people and learned to fire those who weren't. She bet the farm on editor Ben Bradlee. . . ."[2]

Years later Katharine Graham would recall those first days running *The Washington Post*:

> Left alone, no matter at what age or under what circumstance, you have to *remake* your life. The inner turmoil continued. Always in my mind was the climax of the inner years of secret struggle with Phil's illness, the shock of the suicide, the loss, and the eternal questions about why and what next. . . .
>
> I couldn't stop reliving the awful moment of the gun going off, my springing up, racing downstairs, and finding him. The scene replayed in my head until I thought I might be going mad. It took a long time to get through that. To this day, a gun going off or any loud bang affects me profoundly.[3]

When Katharine Graham was asked how she had survived in the rugged media business as a widow she answered, "What I essentially did was to put one foot in front of the other, shut my eyes, and step off the edge. The surprise was that I landed on my feet."[4]

Imagining Your Future as a Survivor

What does your future look like? You may not ever be asked to run a company, but Graham's advice is useful whatever the challenges or circumstances you are facing. You too can live a faithful life and make things happen in your arena. In the end, Graham found a way to make the demands placed on her after her husband's death empowering. She writes, "I had to reshape my life, to give it some new form that would serve not merely to fill my days but to give some real meaning" to her long years as a survivor.[5]

In eulogizing Katharine Graham at the National Cathedral, John

Danforth began, "Mrs. Graham was often described as the most power-ful woman in the world." Though Graham herself would dismiss such accolades, her strength to build a future that sustained her and served her fellow citizens is indisputable. Despite tragedy she had "lived a faithful life," and she made remarkable things happen in our world.[6]

Getting a Future out of Your Past

Humans cannot live without hope. A sense of hopelessness and helplessness menace like tag team wrestlers who "double team" and pummel an opponent in the ring. Do you hope that good things will happen? Do you have curiosity about the near future? Phillips Brooks, the Episcopal bishop and writer, counseled individuals who had expe-rienced great loss, "You must learn. You must let God teach you. The only way to get rid of your past is to get a future out of it."[7]

In leading grief groups, facilitators experience moments when a participant, perhaps off-handedly, offers an insight that they will long remember. One griever in my group said, "I don't want to 'get over it.' I want to get *into* it." So, what is your goal as a survivor? To get "over" this suicide wound, or to get "into" it? If so, how willing are you to learn? to wait? to experience? How willing are you to let God lead you to "a hope and a future," in the prophet Jeremiah's words? (29:11). Are you willing to cling to that goal of finding hope in despair despite the pressure from the well-meaning crowd to "get over it" and to "move on with your life"? Jodie Johnson, a suicide widow, told me, "None of us can heal, unless we learn from this."[8]

Are you willing to wait for the future God has in mind for you? While writing this chapter, I pondered a verse in the writings of the prophet Habakkuk.

> For the revelation awaits an appointed time;
>> it speaks of the end
>> and it will not prove false.
> Though it linger, wait for it;
>> it will certainly come and will not delay. (2:3)

Insert future into that sentence: "For the *future* awaits an appointed time. . . ." That is hard to hear in a culture that snaps up the latest success motivation book that tells you that *you* can make the future happen if you follow this guru's steps or formulas. But God is involved in our lives, and we need to watch for God's hand to show us into our future. Anthony Padovano observed, "We wait for everything that is really worth having. . . ."[9]

While in San Miguel writing chapters of this book, I took a cooking class on making Mexican salsas. The instructor placed a large bowl of dried, shriveled peppers in front of us. She believed those peppers, poor as they looked, had a future. First, she lightly toasted the peppers. Then she placed the peppers in a pan of simmering water. After thirty minutes, she opened the peppers, removed the seeds, and deveined them. Then she packed the peppers into a blender and flipped the switch. Finally, the instructor strained the warm mixture and placed it aside for later.

When students sampled the sauces we had made from that mixture later in the day, I thought back to how the morning began—with a stack of dried-out peppers. A master chef taught us to get a future out of those peppers, something I could not easily have achieved on my own. I did not have all of the understanding or all of the tools needed for the job. But I learned from someone who did.

In the middle of a drought, the prophet Elijah predicted rain. After praying, he sent a servant to scan the horizon toward the sea for rain clouds. Six times the prophet prayed; six times the servant reported that he saw nothing in the sky. But the seventh time, the servant disclosed, "A cloud as small as a man's hand is rising from the sea" (1 Kings 18:44). Within moments, the sky "grew black with clouds, the wind rose, and a heavy rain came on" (v. 45).

What do you see on your emotional and spiritual horizon? More specifically, do you see a rerun of the past, or do you see a future? A God-shaped future? What role will this suicide have in your life? Is there the smallest hope-soaked cloud—perhaps no larger than a man's hand—on your horizon?

Fear of public ridicule troubles almost all survivors. We worry that some may whisper about us, "Her husband killed himself. She *never* got over it!" Such judgments are hurtful and lack charitable insight into the difficult road a survivor travels after a suicide. Yet in truth, some survivors never "get over" the grief of their loss because they never got "into" the futuring, the possibility of a new life after death. They never allowed the interaction of faith and suicide to stir new depth and meaning to their life. We must take responsibility for living beyond this death, and God is a companion who can help us do that.

Jodie Johnson, the surviving wife of a prominent Episcopal bishop who suicided, looked beyond the immediate surroundings of her diocese in Massachusetts. At a certain point she concluded, "I don't want my identity to be totally as the widow of Bishop Johnson. I need to be somebody in addition to that."[10] She was ready to step beyond the past in order to make a future.

In their book *Widowers: The Men Who Are Left Behind*, Scott Campbell and Phyllis Silverman interviewed a group of widowed husbands. From these conversations, the authors identified three primary plateaus in grief. Their construct can apply not just for the grief experiences of widowers. It is also adaptable for suicide grievers.

Healing your wounds,
Repairing your life, and,
Expanding the boundaries of who you are *now*.[11]

For Anson Jones, the last president of the Republic of Texas, the admission of Texas to the United States offered great opportunities. He set his heart on a U.S. Senate seat. (In those days, U.S. senators were elected by the state legislature.) Legislators, however, chose Thomas Jefferson Rusk and Jones's bitter enemy, Sam Houston, to represent their new state. What humiliated Anson Jones was that he did not receive a single vote in the legislature. Despondent at his loss, he left his family at their Brazoria plantation and traveled to Houston. In a room at the Capitol Hotel, on January 9, 1858, Jones fired a bullet into his head, leaving behind a wife and four children. He saw no future for himself.[12]

How does a survivor go about creating a future for their life? We must first deal with the immediate crisis of death. But after some time, repairing slowly begins. We may move back and forth between raw grief and gradual restabilization, able periodically to look up and consider what lies ahead, focused at other times on the loss we have suffered. Jann Fielden comments, "Surviving suicide involves a process of living and grieving that ebbs and flows, changing shape and form over time to eventually give rise to a different way of being-in-the-world."[13]

As awkward as it seems, suicide is in part an invitation to a transformative experience. Victoria Alexander reflected:

> I'm not the same person I was before my mother's death, not only because of her loss but because suicide has become part of the vocabulary of my experience. It has a permanent place at the core of my life, and I am both more vulnerable and stronger for it.[14]

Iris Bolton reflected on the impact of her 20-year-old son's suicide on her husband and herself:

> We now know that we cannot control what happens to us, but we can take charge of how we respond. We can no longer change the destiny of our beloved son, but we can be sure that our lives will be more meaningful, purposeful, compassionate, forgiving, and loving.[15]

Accepting the aftermath of suicide as an opportunity for us to grow as survivors may seem awkward or even sacrilegious. How can anything good come out of such tragedy? Yet other survivors encourage us to consider, when we are ready, to look toward our futures. Julia Cameron paraphrased God's invitation, "Come to me with what you would have transformed," an invitation to bring our devastation into the process of finding a future for ourselves.[16] Alan Jones adds a complementary thought,

In our movement into the mystery of God [where formation takes place] everything that has happened to us is potential gift: our wounds, our disappointments, our idiosyncrasies, and our failures. This is not to glorify pain and sorrow, but to affirm that such things can be transformed into gift.[17]

Jones maintains that faith "requires us to trust the unknown future not because it is safe . . . but because it is God's."[18]

In midlife I have found great strength in a rather obscure passage in Joshua. In chapter twelve, the reader muddles through difficult-to-pronounce names of obscure kings. But, like a hiker on a mountain trail emerging into a photogenic vista, a remarkable verse follows the list: "When Joshua was old and well advanced in years, the Lord said to him, 'You are very old, and there are still very large areas of land to be taken over'" (Joshua 13:1, NIV). God desires a future for us. Actually, I prefer a rendition I've heard that matches no translation I can find: "Behold you are very old . . . *but there is yet much land to be conquered.*" Something about a "Behold" is good for a survivor's soul. It is as if God said to Joshua, and to us, "Look up!—there is much yet to be accomplished in your spiritual future."

Although his son did not die by suicide, Harold Kushner went into a spiritual wilderness and grappled with the limitations of his faith after his son's death. How, he wondered, could an all-powerful God stand by as Aaron died of *progeria*, a rapid aging disease. Kushner endured what LeRoy Aden calls "a long process of re-examination." This famous rabbi, to whom so many looked for hope and spiritual guidance in their grief, had to revise his understanding of God, the world, and death itself.[19] Out of his wilderness travail came his best-selling examination of the shadows of our spiritual lives—*When Bad Things Happen to Good People.* As he notes in the book, Kushner repeatedly made futuring decisions rather than clinging unshakably to the past.

Rabbi Kushner was not the only parent to lose a son that year. Our lives as humans are filled by sudden losses and tragic turns. Yet not all grieving parents are willing, or as willing, to grapple with their faith, the death of their loved one, and the uncertainty of their lives as survivors long enough to "get a future out of it." God may not lead you to write a book and go on the lecture circuit—although countless millions of people have been blessed by Kushner doing so—but God does want you to make a future in the grief you are living. Could Judy Collins have imagined—days after she buried her son Clark, and as the long shadow of grief fell on her life—that in some distant day she would write *Sanity and Sexuality*, a book that would point many to the possibility of a future after suicide. Collins recently responded to questions on the Internet site Beliefnet, and some correspondents suggested that writing her book must have been painful. "There are very few things you can do with these sorts of experiences except try to share them to hopefully help people," Collins replied.[20]

Looking for ways to help others can be a powerful step into the future. Your future might be sitting in an all-night diner or in a coffee shop listening to a broken parent, spouse, or sibling tell their story and recite their why's. Your future might be sitting in a mutual-help grief support group where the telling of your story inspires future-focus for another griever. In that listening, because of your experience, you will plant a seed that may lead to the next Collins, the next Kushner, or the next you.

Your Future Is Your Life

An important part of a survivor's future is simply to continue living. Through their research, Adina Wrobleski and John McIntosh have raised our awareness of a survivor's risk of suicide in the days following a death. As we might anticipate, this danger shows itself at about the time that community and family support for the survivor wanes.[21] Some may declare, "I cannot live without [Name]." Others would not take their own lives but nevertheless cannot imagine a meaningful future without the person who has died.

You have a future. Though you may not see it in yourself, you have work to do to help others. It is important for you to look up, and to live.

If you find yourself in this situation, wishing to end your own life or unable to imagine life at all, let this become your prayer: "God, help me imagine a future, even without [Name]."

Expanding the Boundaries of My Current Life

We are not finished. As human beings, we are all changing, developing, becoming someone new. All survivors are works-in-progress, and our spiritualities are equally works-in-progress. With this in mind, Molly Fumia identifies two tasks for grievers. First, we must "translate the fear into wisdom."[22] What is our fear, and what wisdom does it contain? Surely Winston Churchill, as England's wartime prime minister, felt fear during the relentless Nazi bombing blitz of London. However, he turned his nation's fear into wisdom—a wisdom that energized the British and eventually led to victory.

God can help us confront our fear. I love to sing a hymn written by Carl Daw, Jr., which goes, "Surely it is God who saves me, trusting him I shall not be afraid."[23] To paraphrase Mr. Daw, survivors could sing, "Surely it is God who *futures* me, I will trust in God and not be afraid." My faith is energized by this conviction: God will never be hamstrung by any circumstance of a life. God will relentlessly work to sculpt meaning out of chaos, whether we have created the chaos by our choices, or whether we have inherited it. The challenge for survivors is to trust a God who is working incognito, within the shadows of our grief and drawing us into our future.

Secondly, Fumia urges us to expand our boundaries. She contends that you expand boundaries when you "allow your woundedness to send you *into* the world rather than withdraw from it." You expand your boundaries when you "allow the wisdom of your solemn experience to inform your heart and send you racing to the side of suffering."[24]

Pastor Frederick Buechner tells a story about the pastoral care offered by his wife's grandfather, Rev. George Shinn. An elderly woman was dying alone, without any family. Rev. Shinn and a physician set out in the middle of the night to find someone who could come and be with the woman. One person insisted that she had to think of her own children; another distrusted two men making such a request in the middle of the night. When they knocked at a third door, the mother of a large number of children stuck her head out of the window and demanded, "Who's there? And what do you want at this time of night?" They described their concern for the dying woman and asked, "Will you come?"

"Sure I'll come, and I'll do the best I can," the mother replied.

Buechner concludes, "And she did come. . . . She did the best she could."[25] You have been wounded, and you deserve time and space to begin slowly healing. Yet a call will certainly come to you, asking you to accompany another hurting person. Will you respond as this mother did? Will you allow your boundaries to expand? Will you help out of your own sorrow?

No More Tears

Out of his grief Robert Benson framed this consoling eulogy for his brother Tom:

> My brother is gone. I am not glad that he is gone, but I am glad that he no longer knows the anguish that he knew. I am glad that at least one of the things to which he has gone is the realization that he was loved far more than he ever really knew here.[26]

There is a future towards which all creation can look, for there will come that day when the great promise of God, so long delayed, will be at last redeemed: "God himself will be with them and be their God. He will wipe away every tear from their eyes. There will be no more death or mourning or crying or pain, for the old order of things has passed away" (Revelation 21:3–4). Given the fact that every 16.6 minutes someone suicides, it is hard to comprehend a deathless day—no more death, no more mourning. No more suicide!

I long for the fulfillment of that promise. I am impatient for God's healing of creation. On that day, however long the line, I want to stand until that promise is redeemed. I believe that God keeps promises, and I believe that God will keep this ultimate promise too. On some distant day you will stand, watching closely to see God signal that it is your time to receive the promise.

Until that time, there is a more immediate future that calls us. We wait for God's final healing of the world, but in the meantime someone needs you, today, to scan the horizon for a cloud of hope, of God's promise to open for us a way forward. "God, help me do the best I can" is a prayer for hope-making, for expanding boundaries, for conquering the emotional and spiritual landscapes of grief and fear—for getting a future out of the past.

Conclusion

Alan Jones, who counseled many suicide survivors in his long service as a priest, offers three questions for imaging a future:

1. Do I believe that my life comes to me as a gift and that there is in me a terrific thing?
2. Am I, in the middle of my own struggles, daring enough to ask for help, seek guidance, and cultivate friendships?
3. Am I sincere in wanting to respond to my longing for God, especially when I know and fear the revolutionary changes that may be involved?[27]

How you answer those three questions will shape the future you experience.

Sometimes, it takes a veteran who has walked the walk to summarize an issue succinctly. Iris M. Bolton is such a survivor:

My ten years of healing have also taught me something else about the future. I know that this experience can provide the fertilizer for growth and for the unfolding of a new awareness and appreciation of life and its treasures. Fertilizer comes from manure, from waste. It smells bad; it stinks. But given time, it can sweeten the earth and can help to produce wheat, which can be baked into bread and smells good. It comes full circle, providing food and nourishment—and comfort.[28]

Reflection: Think of the grief through which you are living. Where in it do you sense a future taking root?

Prayer: God, Future-giver, after all I have been through it is hard to believe in a future without [Name]. Give me courage to imagine a future that only you can bring. Amen.

Chapter 11

Anticipating That Distant Day

I choose to believe in a tomorrow
that is God-shaped and God-timed,
peopled with those I have loved
and those who have loved me.
And all the wounds that have dominated my narrative
and the narratives of those I have loved
will, at last, be wholly healed.
And we will dance.
Oh, yes, we will dance!

How could we ever sing God's song in this wasteland?
—Eugene Peterson, Psalm 137:4, The Message[1]

As Captain Meriwether Lewis stood scanning the Pacific after eighteen months of laboriously trudging across the North American continent, he stood where no white man had ever stood. Skeptics had doubted when Thomas Jefferson, his friend, had appointed him to co-lead the expedition. How could this undertaking be successful? Now, it was time to head back to Washington, and to begin the task of preparing the journals of the expedition for publication. He and his men arrived triumphantly in Washington, D.C. on December 28, 1806. Mission accomplished. To cap their success, President James Madison, at Jefferson's behest, appointed Lewis to be Governor of the Territory of Upper Louisiana in Saint Louis.

The glory of the moment, however, would not last. Soon there were bureaucratic battles, and allegations between Lewis and William

Eustis, the Secretary of War, over expenditures and reimbursement of funds. Quarrels broke out with government agents and citizens in Saint Louis. Creditors were seeking to seize Lewis's land assets, and his reputation.

In September 1809, Lewis set out for Washington to settle the dispute and reclaim his mangled name. On the trail, a servant accompanying him noted that Lewis "appeared at times deranged in mind." On October 10, the two men arrived at an inn about seventy miles south of Nashville. Sometime after midnight, Lewis fired two bullets—one grazed his skull, the other pierced his chest. He reportedly said, "I have done the business my good Servant give me some water" and "I am no coward; but I am so strong, [it is] hard to die."[2]

Two centuries later some would claim that Lewis had been murdered—finding it impossible to believe that such a hero could suicide. But the truth was evident to Lewis's contemporaries. William Clark, the other leader of the famed western expedition, was also traveling to Washington when word reached him. He learned in Kentucky of Lewis's death from his brother-in-law. Clark confessed the news was "a turble Stroke to me in every respect."[3]

The death created an immediate crisis. Where were the trunks containing the journals and scientific specimens from the expedition? Clark concluded, "I fear O' I fear the weight of his mind has overcome him, what will be the Consequence?"[4] So disturbing was Lewis's death that Clark altered his travel plans and set out for Monticello to secure Jefferson's guidance and support.

Two centuries later survivors ask variations of Clark's powerful question: "What will be the Consequence?" What will be the consequence of *this* suicide? For most, the days, months, and years after a suicide are a dark spiritual and emotional wasteland, one full of unresolved questions and unanswered wonderings.

But God does not intend this place to be a permanent settlement. Survivors Judy Collins, Albert Hsu, Joan Rivers, Peter Selwyn, Iris Bolton, Michael Mayne, Nan Zastrow, and Susan Chance chose not to be permanent residents of the wasteland created by suicide. These survivors extracted a gift from their loss in actions and words that have comforted others who now, too, know the shadow of grief.

The psalmist captured the reality we face: "Even though I walk through the valley of the shadow of death . . ." (Psalm 23:4). Until writing this manuscript I had never reflected on the power of the word *through*. Our grief is no permanent encampment. Our experience as survivors is an expedition of the soul—though this journey is no less rigorous than that of Lewis and Clark. Yet we do not travel alone. Many survivors have found confidence in the psalmist's reassurance: "I will fear no evil, for you are with me" (v. 4). We are accompanied, even as we trek through the land of the long shadow.

We are confronted with the challenge of living, of finding a future for ourselves as survivors. In this challenge, there is hope. Judy Collins reflects, "Hard times can bring out the best in us, and force us to find the light, to reinvest/invent ourselves, to face things that we would never have chosen to face."[5] Struggles can become tutors for an enlarged human spirit. Collins insists that accepting such challenges is by no means easy or comfortable. She writes, "There are so many deep wounds that can paralyze the heart and even stop your feet from moving toward the help that might be there."[6] Yet with God's help you can imagine the land beyond the long shadow.

Meriwether Lewis had neither wife nor children to mourn him. If you had told him, "Generations yet unborn will know you and celebrate your gift to the nation. Students at all levels of the educational process will study you. Historians and biographers and naturalists will admire your courage and discipline. A postage stamp will honor you and your expedition," he could not have heard you in those distressed final weeks of his life. Stephen Ambrose, a historian of Lewis and a suicide survivor, summed up his legacy:

> He wound up a suicide. He was an alcoholic. He was a manic depressive. He was a speculator in lands and lost his shirt. The government was calling in his chits and denying his expenses. . . . [H]e was broken in every way by the time he died, but he's one of our greatest national heroes.[7]

Would we be one nation "from sea to shining sea" if it had not been for this man's perseverance? No wonder that Jefferson called his friend a man of "of undaunted courage." Would we have known the details of the expedition if Clark, a survivor, had not persisted in their publication?[8] Lewis and Clark had gone far together, only to be separated suddenly by suicide. Yet the partnership of these two men—one who suicided, one who survived—continued after Lewis's death. Their work came to fruition, and we benefit from its legacy still today.

Great women and great men—even those of undaunted courage—suicide. Ordinary women, men, children, adolescents, and elders suicide. Never do we know how much psychache one human spirit can tolerate. And we must recognize that those who remain and grieve, the survivors, possess an undaunted courage, too.

Beyond Suicide

Suicide, in the economy of grace, never gets the last word. That assessment belongs to the one John's Gospel calls the life that "was the light of men," a light that shines in the darkness.

In 2002, I was pulpit guest for Dr. Robert Schuller's *Hour of Power*. After he interviewed me, he told in his sermon a story about a little boy, who when lonely, would call the information operator on the telephone. One day he was troubled after finding his pet bird dead. The operator comforted him by saying, "There are other worlds in which to sing." Over the years, as the boy became a teen and then a young adult, he would call and chat with the same operator, Sally.

One day when he called, a new operator answered. When the young man asked for Sally the new operator replied, "Are you a friend?" When he answered yes, she told him that the operator had died. Then she asked his name.

"Oh, I have a message for you," she responded when she recognized his name. "She said to tell you if you called, 'There are other worlds in which to sing.'"

In the last conversation I had with my friend Martin before he died, he said, in response to my sadness, "The next time you see me I'll be singing in the choir. Tenor section." Martin knew that there are other worlds in which to sing.

The care and consolation we can offer each other cannot heal all of our pain. I cannot fix your sadness. I cannot fix your grief. But I can tell you that there are other worlds in which to sing. I find hope in a passage from Hebrews: "Women received back their dead," the writer proclaims, speaking of mothers whose sons had died and then were resurrected (Hebrews 11:35). The words are prophetic for us. Hear them in a new context, in the setting of your own life, your own loss. There will come that great day in God's eternity when survivors will receive back their dead. And no joy on earth will match that moment.

Until that day, as a survivor:

COMMIT yourself to keeping your grief.
RESIST answers without cost.
MOVE toward integration of your loss.
EMBRACE surviving as an opportunity.
DARE to cling to a grace sufficient for the demands of today
and thousands of days-yet-to-be.
BELIEVE in things you cannot explain.
TRUST in what you cannot comprehend.
HOPE in a tomorrow on some distant horizon.

Reflection: Time does not heal all wounds. Survivors heal.

Prayer: Strengthener, thank you for grace
as outrageous as I need it to be on the darkest days
when why's dance on my heart and mind.
Strengthen my longing for that distant day
when I and my loved one
will dance in your kingdom.

Notes

Introduction

1. Neimeyer, Robert A. (2000). Searching for the meaning of meaning: Grief therapy and the process of reconstruction. *Death Studies, 24,* 550.

2. Shneidman, Edwin S. (2001). Suicidology and the university: A founder's reflections at 80. *Suicide & Life-Threatening Behavior, 31*(1), 1–8.

3. Henson, John. (2004). Good as new: A radical retelling of the scriptures. New York: O Books, 343.

4. Shneidman, Founder's reflections, 8.

5. Ashenburg, Katherine. (2004). *Mourner's dance: What we do when people die.* New York: North Point Press, 6.

6. Jordan, John R. (2001). Is suicide bereavement different? A reassessment of the literature. *Suicide & Life-Threatening Behavior, 31*(1), 91–102.

7. Alexander, Victoria. (1991). *Words I never thought to speak: Stories of life in the wake of suicide.* New York: Lexington Books, 4.

Chapter 1: The Face of Suicide

1. Karff, Samuel E. (2005). *Permission to believe: Finding faith in troubled times.* Nashville, TN: Abingdon, 116–117.

2. Truman, Margaret. (1986). *Bess W. Truman.* New York: Macmillan, 18.

3. *Ibid.,* 234.

4. *Ibid.,* 235.

5. Phillips, M. R., Li, X., & Zhang, Y. (2002, 9 March). "Suicide rates in China, 1995–1999." *The Lancet.* (New York: Elsevier, 1823) vol. 359, issue 9309.

6. Torpy, Janet M. (2005, 25 May). Suicide. *Journal of the American Medical Association,* 2293(20), 2558.

7. American Medical Association. (2004, 3 March). Suicide in older persons. *Journal of the American Medical Association,* 1158. hama.ana.assn.org/cgi/content/full.

8. National Center for Health Statistics, Centers for Disease Control, U.S. Department of Health and Human Services. (2002). http://www.cdc .gov/nchs/fastats/suicide.htm (Accessed 2005, 25 July).

9. D'Augelli, A. R., Hershberger, S. L., & Pilkington, N. W. (2001). Suicidality patterns and sexual orientation-related factors among lesbian, gay, and bisexual youth. Suicide & Life-Threatening Behavior, 31(3), 250.

10. Ibid.

11. Resnick, M. D., Bearman, P., Blum, R. W., et al. (1997). Protecting adolescents from harm: Findings from the National Longitudinal Study on Adolescent Health, Journal of the American Medical Association, 278, 823.

12. Bearman, Peter S., & Moody, James. (2004). Suicide and friendships among American adolescents. American Journal of Public Health, 94(1), 89.

13. Ackerman, G. L. (1993). A congressional view of youth suicide. American Suicide, 48, 183–184.

14. Resnick, et al. Protecting adolescents from harm, 823.

15. American Association of Suicidology. (2004). Youth Suicide Fact Sheet, 3.

16. Ibid.

17. Ibid.

18. Schernhammer, Eva. (2005, 16 June). Taking their own lives—the high rate of physician suicide. The New England Journal of Medicine, 352(24), 2474; Torre, Dario M., Wang, Nae-Yuh, Meoni, Lucy A., Young, J. Hunter, Klag, Michael J., & Ford, Daniel E. (2005). Suicide compared to other causes of mortality in physicians. Suicide & Life-Threatening Behavior, 35(2), 146–153.

19. Black, D. W., & Winoker, G. (1990). Suicide and psychiatric diagnosis. In S. J. Blumenthal & D. J. Kupfer (Eds.), Suicide over the life cycle: Risk factors, assessment and treatment of suicidal patients (pp. 135–153). New York: American Psychiatric Press.

20. NIMH, www.nimh.nih.gov/suicideprevention/suicidefaq.cfm.

21. Ibid

22. Wrobleski, Adina, & McIntosh, John L. (1987). Problems of suicide survival: A survey report. Israeli Journal of Psychiatry and Related Sciences, 24, 139.

23. Schernhammer, Taking their own lives, 2474.

24. Feuer, Alan. (1998, 21 July). Drawing a bead on a baffling endgame: Suicide by cop. New York Times, Section 4.3.

25. O'Connor, Sandra Day. (1992). 505 U.S. 833, Planned Parenthood of Southeastern Pennsylvania vs. Casey, 850.

26. Donne cited in Jamison, Kay Redfield. (1999). *Night falls fast: Understanding suicide.* New York: Vintage, 17.

27. Alvarez, Alfred. (1973). *The savage god.* New York: Basic Books, 155–156.

28. Mark Chafee cited in Hennessy, Tom. (2004, December). Part seven, Special Report: Suicide: Out of the darkness. *Press-Telegram* (Long Beach, CA), 19.

29. Nelson-Becker, Holly B. (2004). Spiritual, religious, nonspiritual, and nonreligious narratives in marginalized older adults: A topology of coping styles. *Journal of Religion, Spirituality, & Aging, 17,* 36.

30. American Association of Suicidology. (2004, 30 August). Survivors of Suicide Fact Sheet, 1.

31. Wrobleski, Adina. (1991). *Suicide: Survivors—A guide for those left behind.* Minneapolis, MN: Afterwards Publishing, 49.

32. Crosby, Alex E., & Sacks, Jeffrey J. (2002). Exposure to suicide: Incidence and association with suicidal idealization and behavior: United States, 1994. *Suicide and Life-Threatening Behavior, 32,* 321–328.

33. Wead, Doug. (2003). *All the presidents' children: Triumph and tragedy in the lives of America's first families.* New York: Altra, 253.

34. Bolton, Iris M., with Mitchell, Curtis. (1983, 2001). *My son . . . my son . . . A guide to healing after death, loss, or suicide.* Roswell, GA: Bolton Press Atlanta, 14.

35. Logan, Joshua. (1976). *Josh: My up and down, in and out life.* New York: Delacorte, 3.

36. Selwyn, Peter A. (1998). *Surviving the fall: The personal journey of an AIDS doctor.* New Haven, CT: Yale University Press, 113.

37. *Ibid.,* 107.

38. *Ibid.*

39. Fielden, Jann M. (2003). Grief as a transformative experience: Weaving through different lifeworlds after a loved one has completed suicide. *International Journal of Mental Health Nursing, 12,* 74–85.

40. Jamison, Kay Redfield. (1999). *Night falls fast: Understanding suicide.* New York: Vintage, 293.

41. Rivers, Joan. (1997). *Bouncing back: I've survived everything . . . and I mean everything and you can, too.* New York: HarperCollins, 20.

42. Allison, C. Fitzsimmons. (2005, 21 July). Trustworthy gentleman [Funeral homily for William Westmoreland]. Charleston, South Carolina, Saint Michael's Church.

43. Shaw, Thomas M. (1995, 19 January). Homily [Funeral for Bishop David E. Johnson]. Boston, MA, Trinity Church.

44. Sandell-Berg, Caroline V. (1972). "Children of the heavenly father," In *Worship in song.* Kansas City, MO: Lillenas, 161. [Public domain]

45. Alexander, Cecil Francis. (1985). "Jesus calls us." *The Hymnal 1982.* New York: Church Publishing 1982, 549. [Public domain]

Chapter 2: Asking Why, Saying Goodbye

1. Neimeyer, Robert A. (1998). *Lessons of loss: A guide to coping.* New York: McGraw-Hill/Primis Custom Printing, 54.

2. Ambrose, Stephen E. (2002). *To America: Personal reflections of an historian.* New York: Simon & Schuster, 158.

3. Van Dongen, Carol J. (1990). Agonizing questioning: Experiences of survivors of suicide victims. *Nursing Research, 39*(4), 224–229. See also Glasser, B. G., & Straus, A. L. (1967). *The discovery of grounded theory: Strategies for qualitative research.* New York: Aldine (1980). Grounded theory methodology: Its uses and processes. *Image, 12*(1), 20–23.

4. Wertheimer, Alison. (1991/2003). *A special scar: The experiences of people bereaved by suicide.* 2nd ed. Philadelphia: Brunner-Rutledge/Taylor & Francis, 74.

5. *Ibid.* citing Shneidman, Edwin S. (1993). *Psychache: A clinical approach to self-destructive behavior.* Northvale, NJ: Jason Aronson, 93.

6. Staudacher, Carol. (1987). *Beyond grief: A guide for recovering from the death of a loved one.* Berkeley, CA: New Harbinger Publications, 179.

7. Clinton, Bill. *My life.* New York: Knopf, 532.

8. Jordan, John R. (2005, 27 October). Suicide awareness: Prevention, intervention and postvention. The American Academy of Bereavement 2005 National Conference. Phoenix, AZ.

9. *Ibid.*

10. Walter, Tony. (2005). Mediator deathwork. *Death Studies, 29,* 408.

11. *Ibid.*

12. Clinton, *My life,* 532.

13. No endnote information is given for this quote.

14. DeSalvo, Louise. (1996). *Vertigo: A memoir.* New York: Dutton, 245.

15. *Ibid.,* 246.

16. Collins, Judy. (2003). *Sanity & grace: A journey of suicide, survival, & strength.* New York: Jeremy Tarcher, 70.

17. Zastrow, Nan. (1997). *Blessed are they that mourn: An observation about what hurts and what heals.* Wausau, WI: Roots and Wings, Ltd., 20.

18. Dravecky, David, Dravecky, Jan, with Gire, Ken. (1992). *When you can't come back: A story of courage and grace*. Grand Rapids, MI: Zondervan, 114.

19. No endnote information is given for this quote.

20. *The Book of Common Prayer and administration of the sacraments and other rites and ceremonies of the church*. (1979). New York: Seabury Press, 862.

21. Rilke, Rainer Maria. (2001). *Letters to a Young Poet*. New York: Modern Library, 35.

22. Benson, Robert. (2004). *A Good Life: Benedict's guide to everyday joy*. Brewster, MA: Paraclete Press, 71.

Chapter 3: Permitting Ourselves to Grieve and Survive

1. Neimeyer, Robert A. (1998). *Lessons of loss: A guide to coping*. New York: McGraw-Hill/Primis Custom Publishing, 88.

2. Morris, Sylvia Jukes. (1980). *Edith Kermit Roosevelt: Portrait of a First Lady*. New York: Coward, McCann & Geoghegan, 507.

3. Rennehan, Edward J., Jr. (1998). *The lion's pride: Theodore Roosevelt & his family in peace and war*. New York: Oxford University Press, 232.

4. Caroli, Betty Boyd. (1998). *The Roosevelt women*. New York: Basic Books, 297.

5. Hewitt, John. H. (1980). *After suicide*. Louisville, KY: Westminster Press, 51.

6. Graham, Katharine. (1997). *Personal history*. New York: Vantage, 531–532

7. Nuland, Sherwin B. (1994). *How we die*. New York: Knopf, 158.

8. Johnson, Jodie. (2005, 4 August). Personal communication.

9. Oliver, Charles M. (1999). *Ernest Hemingway, A to Z: The essential reference to the life and work*. New York: Facts on File, 315.

10. Jamison, *Night falls fast*, 168.

11. Johnson, Jodie. (2005, 4 August). Personal communication.

12. Chance, Sue. (1992). *Stronger than death: When suicide touches your life*. New York: Norton, 74.

13. Baugher, Bob, & Jordan, Jack. (2002). *After suicide loss: Coping with your grief*. Newcastle, WA: Bob Baugher, 5.

14. Murphy, Shirley A., Johnson, L. Clark, & Lohan, Janet. (2003). Challenging the myths about parents' adjustment after the sudden, violent death of a child. *Journal of Nursing Scholarship, 35*(4), 359–364.

15. Shneidman, Edwin S. (1996). *The suicidal mind*. New York: Oxford University Press, 4.

16. Doka, Kenneth. (1989). "Disenfranchised grief." In Kenneth Doka

(Ed.), *Disenfranchised grief: Recognizing hidden sorrow* (pp. 3–11). Lexington, MA: Lexington Books, 4.

17. Hennessy, Tom. (2004, December). Part Four, Special Report: Suicide: Out of the darkness. *Press-Telegram* [Long Beach, CA], 11.

18. Wicks, Robert J. (2003). *Riding the Dragon: 10 Lessons for Inner Strength in Challenging Times.* Notre Dame, IN: Sorin Books, 45.

19. Mayne, Michael. (1998). *Pray, love, remember.* London: Darton, Longman, & Todd, 57.

20. *Ibid.*

21. *Ibid.,* 58.

22. *Ibid.,* 59.

23. Havergal, Frances Ridley. (1985). Take my life and let it be. *The Hymnal 1982.* New York: Church Publishing 1982, 707. [Public domain]

Chapter 4: Reconstructing Meaning After Suicide

1. Neimeyer, Robert A. (1998). *Lessons of loss: A guide to coping.* New York: McGraw-Hill/Primis Custom Publishing, 92.

2. Logan, Joshua. (1976). *Josh: My up and down, in and out life.* New York: Delacorte, 386–387.

3. Neimeyer, *Lessons of loss,* 92.

4. Neimeyer, Robert A. (2000). Searching for the meaning of meaning: Grief therapy and the process of reconstruction. *Death Studies, 24,* 554.

5. Fonda, Jane. (2005). *My life so far.* New York: Random House, 22.

6. *Ibid.,* 25.

7. *Ibid.,* 26.

8. *Ibid.,* x.

9. Neimeyer, Searching for the meaning, 550.

10. Bolton, Iris M., with Mitchell, Curtis. (1983/2001). *My son . . . my son . . . A guide to healing after death, loss, or suicide.* Roswell, GA: Bolton Press, 16.

11. *Ibid.,* 17.

12. *Ibid.,* 72.

13. *Ibid.*

14. Fonda, *My life so far,* 29.

15. *Ibid.,* 30.

16. Buechner, Frederick. (1992). *Listening to your life: Daily meditations with Frederick Buechner.* Ed. George Connor. San Francisco: HarperSanFrancisco, 324.

17. Hsu, Albert Y. (2002). *Grieving a suicide: A loved one's search for comfort, answers, & hope.* Downers Grove, IL: InterVarsity Press, 10.

18. Neimeyer, *Lessons of loss*, 93.

19. Karff, Samuel E. (2005). *Permission to believe: Finding faith in troubled times*. Nashville, TN: Abingdon, 35.

20. *Ibid.*, 117.

21. Buechner, *Listening to your life*, 318–319.

22. Buechner, Frederick. (1999). *The eyes of the heart*. San Francisco: HarperSanFrancisco, 23–24.

23. Cowper, William. (1985). "God moves in a mysterious way." *The Hymnal 1982*. New York: Church Publishing 1982, 677. [Public domain]

Chapter 5: Surviving Suicide's Assault on Our Assumptions and Values

1. Neimeyer, Robert A. (1998). *Lessons of loss: A guide to coping*. New York: McGraw-Hill/Primis Custom Publishing, 87.

2. See Tavenner, Mary Hilaire. (2001). *A portrait of Helen Steiner Rice*. Pittsburgh, PA: Dorrance.

3. Neimeyer, *Lessons of loss*, 87–88.

4. Parkes cited in *Ibid*.

5. *Ibid.*, 88.

6. Hsu, Albert Y. (2002). *Grieving a suicide: A loved one's search for comfort, answers, & hope*. Downers Grove, IL: InterVarsity Press, 10.

7. Baugher and Jordan, *After suicide loss*, 32.

8. Collins, Judy. (2003). *Sanity & grace: A journey of suicide, survival, & strength*. New York: Jeremy Tarcher, 72.

9. Baugher, Bob, & Jordan, Jack. (2002). *After suicide loss: Coping with your grief*. Newcastle, WA: Bob Baugher & Jordan, 44.

10. Jamison, Kay Redfield. (1999). *Night falls fast: Understanding suicide*. New York: Vintage, 19.

11. Smedes, Lewis B. (1986). *Choices: Making right decisions in a complex world*. San Francisco: Harper & Row, 3.

12. Carson, Steven Lee. (2005, August). American biography: Alice Roosevelt Longworth. *American History, 40*(3), 40.

13. Roosevelt, Eleanor. (1960) *You Learn by Living*. New York: Harper.

Chapter 6: Rehabilitating Judas

1. Neimeyer, Robert A. (Ed.). (2001). *Meaning reconstruction & the experience of loss*. Washington, DC: American Psychological Association, xi.

2. Priest's diary details Jacqueline Kennedy's grief. (203, 13 November). *The Kansas City Star*, A2.

3. Reed, David A. (2005). "Saving Judas"—a social scientific approach to Judas' suicide in Matthew 27:3-10. *Biblical Theological Bulletin, 35*(2), 57.

4. Whelan, Caroline F. (1993). Suicide in the ancient world: A re-examination of Matthew 27:3-10. LAVAL, 505–522.

5. Allison, C. Fitzsimmons. (2005, 21 July). Trustworthy gentleman: [Funeral homily for William Westmoreland]. Charleston, South Carolina, Saint Michael's Church.

6. Klassen, William. (1992). Judas Iscariot in David Noel Freedman (Ed.), *The Anchor Bible Dictionary*, Vol. 3. New York: Doubleday, 1092.

7. Spong, John Shelby. (2005). *The sins of scripture: Exposing the Bible's texts of hate to reveal the God of love.* San Francisco: HarperSanFrancisco, Scripture, 200–201.

8. Essex, Barbara J. (2005). *Bad boys of the New Testament: Exploring men of questionable virtue.* Cleveland, OH: Pilgrim Press, 84.

9. Reed, "Saving Judas," 53.

10. Farrell, Bernadette. (1992). "O God, You Search Me." Portland, OR: Oregon Catholic Press. Used by permission.

11. Faber, Frederick William. (1985). *The Hymnal 1982.* New York: Church Publishing 1982, 469. [Public domain]

12. Bridges, Matthew. (1985). "Crown him with many crowns." *The Hymnal 1982.* New York: Church Publishing 1982, 494. [Public domain]

13. *The Catholic Catechism:* 2283. (1997). New York: Doubleday, 609.

14. Long, Kimberly Bracken. (2005). "Who are these people?" Revelation 7:9-17. *Journal for Preachers, 28*(3), 28. Long quotes Revelation 14:7, *The Revised English Bible.* (1989). New York: Oxford University Press.

Chapter 7: Praying Your Grief

1. Ritter, William A. (2004). *Take the dimness of my soul away: Healing after a loved one's death.* Harrisburg, PA: Morehouse Publishing, 33.

2. Fonda, Peter. (1998). *Don't tell Dad.* New York: Hyperion, 45.

3. Neader, Joachim. (1985). "Praise to the Lord, the Almighty." *The Hymnal 1982.* New York: Church Publishing 1982, 390. [Public domain]

4. Rupp, Joyce. (1988). *Praying our goodbyes.* Notre Dame, IN: Ave Maria Press, 79.

5. John Shelby Spong. (2003, March 24). Lecture series. First United Methodist Church, Omaha.

6. Hugo, Victor, cited in Pollock, Constance, & Pollock, Daniel. (1996). *The book of uncommon prayer.* Dallas, TX: Word, 81.

7. Scriven, Joseph. (1972). "What a friend we have in Jesus." In *Worship in Song.* Kansas City, MO: Lillenas Publishing Company, 123. [Public domain]

8. Abraham Lincoln cited in Wirt, Sherwood Eliot, & Beckstrom, Kersten (Eds.). (1982). *Topical encyclopedia of living quotations*. Minneapolis, MN: Bethany House, 183.

9. *The Book of Common Prayer and administration of the sacraments and other rites and ceremonies of the church*. (1979). New York: Seabury Press, 862.

10. James Kimpton quoted in Gallagher, Winifred. (2001). *Spiritual genius: The mastery of life's meaning*. New York: Random House, 12.

11. Vance Havner cited in Zadra, Dan, with Woodard, Marcia (Eds.). (1999). *Forever remembered*. Seattle, WA: Compendium, 54.

12. John Bunyan cited in Ward, Hannah, & Wild, Jennifer (Eds.) (1997). *The Doubleday Christian quotation collections*. New York: Doubleday, 113.

13. Rosten, Leo. (1987). *Leo Rosten's treasury of Jewish quotations*. New York: Bantam, 364.

14. Grumbach, Doris. (1991). *Coming into the end zone*. New York: W. W. Norton, 57.

15. Charles Williams cited in Lewis, C. S. (1946, 1966). Preface. In Dorothy Sayers, J. R. R. Tolkien, C. S., Lewis, A. O. Barfield, Gervase Mathew, & W. H. Lewis, *Essays presented to Charles Williams* (pp. vi–xiv). Grand Rapids, MI: William B. Eerdmans, xiii.

16. Bastis, Madeline Ko-i. (1999, 12 March). *Adapting traditional Buddhist meditation practices for the dying and bereaved*. Workshop presented at the Association for Death Education and Counseling, San Antonio, TX.

17. Rabbinical Assembly. (1998). *Siddur Sim Shalom for Shabbat and festivals*. [No place of publication identified.] The United Synagogue of Conservative Judaism, 184.

18. Kaddish adapted from Kolatch, Alfred J. (1993). *The Jewish mourner's book of why*. Middle Village, NY: Jonathan David, 332.

19. Unruh, D. (1983). Death and personal history: Strategies of identity preservation. *Social Problems, 30*(3), 349.

20. Tennyson, Alfred Lord. (1971). The passing of Arthur. In Robert W. Hill, Jr. (Ed.), *Tennyson's Poetry: Authoritative texts, juvenilia and early responses, criticism*. (1971). New York: Norton, 429.

21. Niebergall, A. & Lathrop, Gordon. (1986). Burial: Lutheran. In J. G. Davies (Ed.). *The new Westminster dictionary of liturgy and worship* (pp. 124–127). Philadelphia: Westminster, 125.

22. Cited in Wieseltier, Leon. (1998). *Kaddish*. New York: Knopf, 192.

23. *The Book of Common Prayer*, 862.

24. Rupp, 1988.

25. Donne, John. (1662). Christmas sermon, 1662. http://www.msgr.ca/mgr-3'john_donne_sermon_10.htm. (Accessed 31 October 2005).

26. *The Book of Common Prayer,* 1979, 481.

27. Williamson, Marianne. (1994). *Illuminata: Thoughts, prayers, rites of passage.* New York: Random House, 120.

28. How, William Walsham. (1985). "For all the saints." *The Hymnal 1982.* New York: Church Publishing 1982, 287. [Public domain]

29. *Book of Hours,* 1514, cited in Batchelor, Mary (Ed.). (1992/1996). *The Doubleday prayer collection.* New York: Doubleday, 460.

30. Tennyson, Alfred Lord. (1971). In memoriam. In Robert W. Hill, Jr. (Ed.), *Tennyson's Poetry: Authoritative texts, juvenilia and early responses, criticism.* New York: Norton, 122.

Chapter 8: Forgiving

1. Ritter, William A. (2004). *Take the dimness of my soul away: Healing after a loved one's death.* Harrisburg, PA: Morehouse Publishing, 49.

2. Hotchner, A. E. (1999). *Papa Hemingway.* New York: Carroll & Graf, 292.

3. Linn-Gust, Michelle. (2001). *Do they have bad days in heaven? Surviving the suicide loss of a sibling.* Albuquerque, NM: Chellehead Works, 65.

4. *Ibid.,* 14.

5. Shreve, Anita. (1998/1999). *The pilot's wife.* Boston, MA: Back Bay, 289.

6. Wroblecki, Adina, & McIntosh, John L. (1987). Problems of suicide survival: A survey report. *Israeli Journal of Psychiatry and Related Sciences,* 24, 139.

7. Chance, Sue. (1992). *Stronger than death: When suicide touches your life.* New York: Norton, 18.

8. *Ibid.,* 19.

9. Fielden, Jann M. (2003). Grief as a transformative experience: Weaving through different lifeworlds after a loved one has completed suicide. *International Journal of Mental Health Nursing,* 12, 78.

10. *Ibid.,* 79.

11. Jordan, Jack. (2005, 27 October). Suicide awareness: Prevention, intervention and postvention. The American Academy of Bereavement 2005 National Conference, Phoenix, AZ.

12. Lamott, Anne. (2005). *Plan b: Further thoughts on grace.* New York: Riverhead Books, 140.

13. Colt, George Howe. *The enigma of suicide.* New York, Summit, 161–170.

14. www.godhatesfags.com/featured/epics/20050622_denison-iowa-epic.html.

15. Hsu, Albert Y. (2002). *Grieving a suicide: A loved one's search for comfort, answers, & hope.* Downers Grove, IL: InterVarsity Press, 138.

16. Rivers, Joan. (1997). *Bouncing back: I've survived everything . . . and I mean everything and you can, too.* New York: HarperCollins, 56.

17. Hsu, *Grieving a suicide,* 137.

18. *Ibid.,* 103.

19. Do we still need hell? (2003, 4 October). *The Christian Century,* 5.

20. Smedes, Lewis B. (2000, 10 July). Is suicide unforgivable? *Christianity Today,* 44(8), 61.

21. *Bad Days in Heaven,* 85.

Chapter 9: Investing in a Charitable Narrative

1. Neimeyer, Robert A. (1998). *Lessons of loss: A guide to coping.* New York: McGraw-Hill/Primis Custom Publishing, 94.

2. Angelo, Bonnie. (2005). *First families: The impact of the White House on their lives.* New York: William Morrow, 64.

3. Davis, Patti. (2004). *The long goodbye.* New York: Knopf.

4. Shneidman, Edwin S. (1996). *The suicidal mind.* New York: Oxford University Press, 144.

5. Coryell, Deborah Morris. (1997/2004). *Healing through the shadow of loss.* Rochester, VT: Healing Arts Press, 83.

6. Hauser, Marilyn J. (1987). Special aspects of grief after a suicide. In Edward J. Dunne, John McIntosh, & Karen Dunne-Maxim (Eds.), Suicide and its aftermath: Understanding and counseling the survivors. New York: Norton, p. 66.

7. Trillin, Calvin. (1993). *Remembering Denny.* New York: Farrar, Straus & Giroux, 210.

8. *Weekly compilation of Presidential documents,* 5/27/1996 [Bill Clinton in *Weekly compilation of Presidential documents,* 5/27/1996. http://www.highbeam.com/library/docfree.asp?DOCID=1G1:18590287&ctr1Info=Roundl (Retrieved 2—5 3 October).]

9. Bolton, Iris M., with Mitchell, Curtis. (1983/2001). *My son . . . my son . . . A guide to healing after death, loss, or suicide.* Roswell, GA: Bolton Press, 41.

10. See Smith, Harold Ivan. (2002). *Grief care guide.* Kansas City, MO: Beacon Hill Press of Kansas City, 121–141.

11. Coryell, *Healing through the shadow of loss,* 126.

12. Bolton, *My son . . . my son*, 64.

13. Coryell, *Healing through the shadow of loss*, 56.

14. Bolton, *My son . . . my son*, 96.

15. Neimeyer, Robert A. (2005). Widowhood, grief, and quest for meaning: A narrative prospect on resilience. In Carr, D., Neese, R. M., & Wortman, Camille B. (Eds.). *Late life widowhood in the United States*. New York: Springer.

Chapter 10: Futuring

1. Neimeyer, Robert A. (1998). *Lessons of loss: A guide to coping*. New York: McGraw-Hill/Primis Custom Publishing, 94.

2. Carlson, Margaret. (2001, 30 July). A woman of substance: Katharine Graham, 1917–1921, 64.

3. Graham, Katharine. (1997). *Personal history*. New York: Vantage, 339.

4. *Ibid.*, 341.

5. Graham, *Personal history*, 622.

6. Danforth, John. (2001, 23 July). Homily. Washington, DC: The National Cathedral.

7. Attributed to Phillips Brooks.

8. Jodie Johnson, Jodie. (2005, 4 August). Personal conversation.

9. Anthony Padovano. (1999). Cited in *The spiritual formation Bible: Growing in intimacy with God through scripture*. Grand Rapids, MI: Zondervan, 1247.

10. Johnson, Jodie. (2005, 4 August). Personal conversation.

11. Campbell, Scott, & Silverman, Phyllis. (1996). *Widowers: The men who are left behind*. Amityville, NY: Baywood, 89.

12. Gambrell, Herbert. (2001). Anson Jones. In Handbook of Texas Outline. http://www.tsha.utexas.edu/handbook/online/articles/JJ/fjo42.html [accessed 2005, June 30].

13. Fielden, Jann M. (2003). Grief as a transformative experience: Weaving through different lifeworlds after a loved one has completed suicide. *International Journal of Mental Health Nursing, 12*, 83.

14. Alexander, Victoria. (1987). *Living through my mother's suicide*. In Edward J. Dunne, John L. McIntosh, & Karen Dunne-Maxim (Eds.), *Suicide and its aftermath: Understanding and counseling the survivors* (pp. 109–120). New York: Norton, 117.

15. Bolton, Iris M., with Mitchell, Curtis. (1983/2001). *My son . . . my son . . . A guide to healing after death, loss, or suicide*. Roswell, GA: Bolton Press, 93.

16. Cameron, Julia. (2004). *Answered prayers: Love letters from the divine faith*. New York: Jeremy P. Tarcher/Putnam, 140.

17. Jones, Alan. (1982). *Exploring spiritual direction: An essay on Christian friendship*. New York: Seabury, 76.

18. *Ibid.*, 42.

19. Aden, LeRoy. (2005). *In life and death: The shaping of faith*. Minneapolis, MN: Augsburg.

20. Collins, Judy. http:www.beliefnet.com/story/ 125/story_13549.html.

21. Wrobleski, Adina, & McIntosh, John L. (1987). Problems of suicide survival: A survey report. *Israeli Journal of Psychiatry and Related Sciences*, 24, 137–142.

22. Fumia, Molly. (1992). *Safe passage: Words to help the grieving hold fast and let go*. Berkeley, CA: Conari Press, 264.

23. Daw, Carl, Jr. (1982/1985). "Surely it is God who saves me." *The Hymnal 1982*. New York: Church Publishing, 679.

24. Fumia, *Safe Passage*, 274.

25. Buechner, Frederick. *Listening to your own life*, 317.

26. Benson, Robert. (1999, 19 May). Personal correspondence.

27. Jones, Alan. (1999). *Exploring spiritual direction*. Cambridge, MA: Cowley, 42.

28. Bolton, *Suicide and its aftermath*, 93.

Chapter 11: Anticipating That Distant Day

1. Peterson, Eugene. (2002). Psalm 137:4, *The Message*. Colorado Springs, CO: NavPress, 818.

2. Tubbs, Stephanie Ambrose, with Jenkinson, Clay Straus. (2003). *The Lewis and Clark companion: An encyclopedic guide to the voyage of discovery*, 194.

3. Jones, Landon. (2005). *William Clark and the shaping of the West*. New York: Hill & Wang, 181.

4. Tubbs & Jenkinson, *The Lewis and Clark companion*, 194.

5. Collins, Judy. (2005). *Morning, noon, and night: Living the creative life*. New York: Tarcher, 145.

6. Collins, Judy. (2003). *Sanity & grace: A journey of suicide, survival, & strength*. New York: Jeremy Tarcher, 84.

7. Ambrose, Stephen. [Online NewsHour, 1996, 20 June, http://www.pbs.org? newshour/gergen/ambrose.html.] Interview with David Gergen.

8. Ambrose, Stephen. [Online NewsHour, 1996, 20 June, http://www.pbs.org? newshour/gergen/ambrose.html.]